Biblical Humility

and

Modern Grace

BY RONALD L. DROWN

Biblical Humility

and

Modern Grace

BY RONALD L. DROWN

Copyright © 2017 All Rights Reserved
Authored By Rev. Ronald L Drown
Published By Ancient Truth Publishing
PO Box 366894, Bonita Springs, FL 34136

Book Cover By: Brittany Schmidt

OTHER BOOKS BY RONALD L DROWN INCLUDE
The Real Jesus and Truth Nuggets

AVAILABLE ON AMAZON OR VISIT THE WEBSITES:

WWW.YAD-EL.COM
WWW.LIGHTHOUSEOFJESUS.ORG

ISBN-13: 978-0-9886616-3-9
ISBN-10: 0988661632

AS SEEN IN CHARISMA MAGAZINE!
SIGN UP TO RECEIVE
THE LORD'S PRAYER IN HEBREW

VISIT WWW.LIGHTHOUSEOFJESUS.ORG

OR SCAN QR CODE BELOW WITH YOUR PHONE
A MONTHLY HEBREW PRAYER WILL BE EMAILED TO
YOU FROM REV RON'S HEBREW PRAYER SERIES
(MP3 DOWNLOAD)

READING TIPS
The following may be used in this book:

Abbreviated letters = Bible Translation Versions, such as;
ASV American Standard Version
ESV English Standard Version
K.J.V. King James Version
NASB New American Standard Bible
NIV New International Version

Other initials used for date reference = BCE, CE, AD
BCE = Before Common Era
CE = Common Era
AD = Anno Domini (used by Christians,
Year of the Lord, since Christ was born)

Table of Contents

PREFACE

In this modern age and time in the United States of America, we are blessed above measure in that we have abundance, when compared to the earthly possessions of our ancestors and forefathers.

For many Americans the standard of living has risen greatly, in the last 50 years. Yet in some regions of the country, there are many who have not been so mightily blessed, and suffer lack in many areas of life. May great and compassionate activities bring assistance to them in their hour of need.

The levels of Christian education have also risen to greater heights in an age of prosperity and blessing, while prosperity preaching and teaching have also become quite influential in American churches.

This is probably due to much media presentation by numerous spokespersons in the religious realm with millions of potential viewers in television and radio audiences. Christian colleges and Universities have also benefited and impacted many youth with excellent teaching material.

There is also a great trickle down impact upon society as a whole. It's noted in worldly institutions as well as in the church world. Space age technology eventually reaches the masses of ordinary people of the lowest strata of society. The lowest groups of any society are always reaching up to a higher living standard.

I have sensed a great need in the American churches to begin to practice **humility**, which is the true balance in individuals and society, which are on the rise from lower strata to higher realms. Christian theology based on New Testament writings, is the true guideline for behavior of believers.

We have numerous examples in the New Testament Church of humility, sobriety, and examples of a humble man in both Testaments. We also have examples of modesty and apostolic writings in that regard. Christians writings also cover such delicate subjects as evolution of grace from the law, while condemning hypocrisy under the law and among grace teachers.

Likewise, we are warned in the New Testament about the trend of lawlessness, which has filtered down from pulpit teachings against "law," and is now seen to be playing out in the streets of modern American cities. Anarchy is not a Christian teaching, yet some who espouse Christ, are involved in such activity.

In some churches the Hollywood mentality

has invaded pulpits and choirs, in order to affect church attendance in a positive manner. But the danger of the ego centered entertainment industry is a huge distraction from subjects like **humility, humbleness, sobriety, modesty,** and any transition or **evolution of grace under the law to grace in the gospel**.

May the words of these writings cause us to all humble ourselves under the mighty hand of God, so that He may exalt us all in due time.

Humility

PART 1

This could be a most unpopular subject among modern American churches; the subject of **denial** of one's self. But we should take a good look at the words and sayings of Jesus, in order to gain an accurate perspective on the matter. It is especially important when our society is promoting much time and effort in lower levels of schooling, to instill in children great values of "self-esteem."

There is a purpose within educational systems to ingrain a positive mindset among children which encourages them to be able to deal with life and its problems from early childhood. This is a good thing, since life itself has many twists and turns, and learning to cope is an important trait for all human beings. Reading, writing, and mathematics are not the only thing a child can begin to learn at an early age. Instilling a positive attitude is needful for the whole of the human character, and some degree of self-confidence is important when problem solving skills become necessary in life.

As a youth I used to wonder now and then; why we were not taught to "think," just as much as to memorize concepts. One day I heard my father say to us boys, in a corrective matter; *use your heads for something beside a hat rack.* It was probably a saying in the old days that elders told their offspring, since I had heard it few times since that day long ago. But, I really focused on those words trying to understand what dad had really said. Eventually I was able to figure it out. He was teaching his young sons to think, and use the common sense God had given them, in practical and sensible ways.

A trend has been noticed among American kids in this day and time, about an extremely self-confident and superior attitude. It is so deeply imbedded in some kids from childhood, that when they become teenagers, they have hopes and dreams beyond what is normal. At times those aspirations in some, border on the realm of egotism. Too much self-esteem can lead to arrogance and lack of courtesy. My wife saw it played out in reality when she was with the school group of American teens, who were travelling in England with school teachers. Although they were strangers travelling in a strange country, you would have thought they owned the world.

They behaved in such a way as to embarrass themselves by rushing onto the subway, crowding into the empty seats, and ignoring the elderly or locals who were left to stand. The kids talked extremely loud, and forgot about polite behavior, so much that my wife was ashamed for them.

It reminds me of a saying about an egotistical person, of whom it was said: I'd like to buy him for what he's worth, and sell him for what he thinks he is worth, and I would be a rich man.

Self-esteem is a good thing, but when there is no balance or practicality, we have nothing left but arrogance. A trend toward haughtiness is the result of lack of balance in the teaching institutions of home and family. Sadly, we have had the same trend developing in Christian churches for a good while. It could have developed due to the lack of teaching about humility in many church groups.

In all cases Christians should set the example in homes, by showing their children a life of submission to the will of God and the word of God. It should not be expected that the church could teach children everything they need to know in a one hour weekly Sunday school session. The home is the place to set a real example. If we as parents behave in a loud, boastful, and arrogant manner in front of the tiny tots, we should not expect anything different from the kids. They also will act just like we have done in front of them.

Humility is a choice to not behave as a carnal and worldly minded person who has no authority above his head. This is seen among Orthodox Jews to some degree in the early Christian church, where Paul wrote to them: ***Every man praying or prophesying with his head covered, dishonors his head*** (1 Corinthians 11:4).

Among Jews like Paul, a belief existed that Christ was the "head" of every man, and the husband was the "head" of the wife. The whole teaching concept was based on humility towards God, since man was made in His image, and the woman should be subject to her husband, since the first woman was made in the image of the man.

However people interpret the verse to be applied in this day and time, the notion of visible humility is quite obvious. Heaven and angels are watching, and whether or not we behave in a humble manner or way of self-denial, is being reported to the Master.

An Israeli guide once told me, as we were

riding the bus in Jerusalem streets: *See all the attractive ladies with the scarves on their heads; that means they have a husband and are under his authority.* They are married! Then he quickly quipped with a smile: *We know who we can flirt with* (author-laughing out loud).

Other interpretations exist in Judaism about a man who walks four cubits with an erect carriage (haughtily), *is as though he pushed against the feet of the Shekinah,* (indication that he is pushing against the Presence of the Almighty). It was said among the sages of Judaism: *If a prophet is proud, or angry, his prophecy departs from him* (Pesachim 66b). Those words of the sages also stress visible humility or self-denial.

Such sayings as those relate the same thing that was written of the man Moses in Numbers 12:3, "***Now the man Moses was very meek, above all the men which were upon the face of the earth.***" Word's like those reveal why God was able to allow Moses to "see" as no other prophet, and to confirm his words, life, and mission to Israel with signs and wonders. That also is written in scripture in Deuteronomy 34:10-12.

According to Numbers 12:6-8, God was able to talk to Moses without vision or dream, but "mouth to mouth." Moses was above all other prophets, in that his extreme meekness or humility, allowed God to speak clearly and without trance, as well as behold the similitude of the Lord. God always honors those who deny self and practice the trait of humility.

Before we go to the words of Jesus about denial of "self," I want to look at the Greek term for "I am," which was written in the Greek Septuagint Version of the Old Testament Hebrew, which was translated around 200-300 BC. A normal way of saying "I am" in Greek is the phrase εγω ειμι, which with English sounds might be <u>ego I-me</u>. Our first word which I have underlined for you, sounds so much like our English "ego." It's English description is; *the self especially as contrasted with another self or the world.*

The next term relates to *I am*, and when given English sounds for the Greek, it can be phonetically sounded as **I Me**, which is a combination of "I" and "me."

When people are overly concerned about "self," English words like *egocentric, egotist, egotism, egoism* all apply to such self-concerns.

In human situations among the Greek speakers, it's simply the way to say **I am**. We hold a different perspective from the words of the bible, as related to the Creator of all things.

His concern and love has always been for his creation and creatures, and after having made them all, His interest is for their well-being. Before God ever made humans, He prepared everything for them, and to sustain mankind and animals.

That is why when we read the account of 6 creative days in the Genesis account, mankind was not created until the 6th day. He wanted everything to be ready made for His creatures. Trees, green grass, plants, fruits, animals, fish, birds, and insects. Aquatic life forms, the sun, moon, and stars to shine at night, with times, and seasons for all things. *His creation of time itself was for humanity's sake, since His habitation was eternity. God was not, and is not self-centered or time regulated.*

It was written of God in the Greek Old Testament in Exodus 3:6; εγω ειμι ο κυριος, *I am the Lord*. The translation term "Lord" which came from *kurios*, has its original source from the parent language of Hebrew. It consists of the sacred Divine and proper name of the God of Israel, which is transliterated with English letters YHVH. English speakers say "Lord." That form of the Divine name is said to appear about 6,823 times in the Old Testament manuscripts. He is not egocentric, but it is known according to some bible verses, that He is a ***Jealous God*** (Exodus 20:5); ***jealous for those whom He***

loves, and for those that love Him. Yet He is tolerant of all people.

This "I am" concept can be offensive to the Lord God when it is out of balance, and produces haughtiness, arrogance, or an egotistical manner among humans. *If the Lord God is able to walk among humans to such an extent that he is unnoticed, then why should humans become haughty and prouder than a peacock, that struts in its own glory?* I find it quite refreshing and a bit humorous, that Jesus, the son of God, **became poor, for our sakes that we through him might be made rich** (see 2 Corinthians 8:9).

The intoxicating effects of success don't always lead humans to honorable behavior, and history supports that notion in many examples. I remember hearing an old adage years ago, and learned to repeat it myself. It went like this: *It's alright to have your head in the clouds, but keep your feet on the ground.* Among our Christian youth groups of years past, we all seemed to understand that saying.

In the interest of balance for youthful enthusiasm, and zeal for the Lord, I want to express a positive note of self-confidence as from the Lord and His word. But we do not desire that people be overly filled with "self-confidence" apart from that which God gives. The true

Christian attitude is expressed first of all in the life and actions of Jesus, secondly, it is made known by His own words as written in the Gospels of Matthew, Mark, Luke and John.

Since Jesus didn't personally write letters or instructions to church groups, we must share his words, as written by certain eyewitnesses of his life, ministry, and teachings, and pass them along to the followers.

We do well to remember the scripture in Hebrews 4:1-2: There it was written that Jesus is the final and last day spokesman, above the prophets, and apostles of time past. In every situation, the words of Jesus have to take precedence, for those who truly believe his mission as given to his followers to *"go you therefore and teach all nations."* Or as in Mark's words; *"preach the gospel,"* and as told by Luke; *"repentance and remission of sins should be preached in his name among all nations beginning at Jerusalem."*

The words of Jesus are the life of the church, and all of that great commission was reported to be given by Jesus for the world.

That command or "Go you" verbiage included, *teaching them to observe all things whatsoever I have commanded you*. Thus the words and sayings of Jesus are instructions from heaven itself, since he is the final and last day spokesman, to the world and the nations. What then did he say about self-denial and humility?

Let's take note of what gospel authors have written for all readers to understand. Some verses which relate to denial of self, will follow as well as verses which actually contain the word *deny*.

It's extremely important as we examine the words of Jesus, that we also see the reason why Jesus chose 12, then 70 apostles, to carry his message to Israel and the nations. They had to be with him from the beginning of his ministry and hear and see what Jesus had done and taught. For they would be the sent one's (apostles). Their words would be what he personally had taught them, and would be sustained by their writings (gospels), and traced back to those accounts (see Acts 1:21-26).

We shall begin with Matthew 10:33. "Whosoever therefore shall confess me before men, him will I confess also before my Father which is in heaven. But whosoever shall deny me before men, him will I also deny before my Father which is in heaven."

Such a statement reveals the importance of

submission to God, by the confession of faith, as spoken in this world. The measure of respect that we give Jesus in this world, determines whether or not he will deny us in the world to come, or before the Father in heaven.

I found a biblical example which clearly shows that the 12 disciples of Jesus, before his death and actual resurrection, denied to having even known him. They later repented.

I'll just write the verses here from Matthew 26:34-35. "I say unto you, That this night before the rooster crow, you shall shalt deny me three [times]. Peter said unto him, Though I should die with you, yet will I not deny you. Likewise also said all the disciples."

It has been often stressed by preachers and teachers that Peter denied the Lord, which is true. But the same verse that says Peter denied, also relates that all the disciples would do the same. Since Peter, was designated as a man of revelation by Jesus, we should expect that he would be more under scrutiny due to leadership position.

It is certain that the confidence level of all the handpicked followers of Jesus, was greatly enhanced due to the abundance of miracles, signs, and wonders they had experienced while being with him.

Approximately 3 years of ministry with Jesus had raised their confidence level to great heights. It is no wonder that when hearing for the first times about his coming betrayal (Matthew 26:22-24), they were unable to accept the prophecy that it would be so.

After all, Jesus had worked so many miracles for others, why would he not be able to deliver himself as he had done for others? The shock of betrayal and denial, was so far removed from the gospel they had learned to preach in synagogues and villages of the Galilee, and did not fit nicely into the kingdom of God theme, which they had learned from Jesus.

That **good tidings** message and the nearness of the hand of God, seemed incompatible with a prophecy of betrayal and denial. It was one thing to be betrayed by one of his followers, but to be denied by them all, would be extremely burdensome for Jesus.

Yet destiny and purpose are not always known by the children or followers of God, nor is full prophetic understanding in the conscious minds of disciples. We should also remember that these coming denials were of a pre-Pentecostal nature.

They had not yet been filled with the Holy Ghost. Although they were privileged to use

Jesus' name, cast out demons, and heal the sick, Jesus would ascend into heaven, and the renewed authority would be granted them by the Spirit of God. No wonder Jesus had told them in Acts 1:4 not to depart Jerusalem until the promise of the Father arrived.

The pre-Pentecostal denial of Jesus, by Peter and the other disciples, can be used as an example of good intentions, but a powerless follow up on one's words (***yet will I not deny you***). The filling of the Holy Spirit enables a person to be a faithful witness for Jesus, and to follow up on the commitment to His cause.

Jesus had forewarned of failure of discipleship in Matthew 16:24, saying; "***If any man will come after me, let him deny himself, and take up his cross, and follow me.***" Our manuscript word for <u>cross</u> is the Greek σταυρος (Strong's #4716) = *stake, pole, cross*).

A Roman execution stake or pole was a place where criminals were executed. There is a huge disagreement about the form of the Roman cross in use at that time, although 5 New Testament verses use the word **tree** in description of the execution site. It was also a **tree** where Judas hung himself according to Matthew 27:5. The Matthew 16:24 verse is the second time the word cross is found in the New Testament, and connects with the terms **deny himself**.

The first time a companion verse uses the word **cross** and comes from the mouth of Jesus, is in   Matthew 10:38. In that verse section (vs. 37), Jesus taught that love of one's father or mother, son or daughter, must not be greater for them, than for Jesus. To love others more than Jesus, was said by him, to make them unworthy of him.

Such words link to the Hebrew quotation and translation of Deuteronomy 6:4.

Shema Yisrael Hashem Eloheynu Hashem Echad.

(שְׁמַע יִשְׂרָאֵל יהוה אֱלֹהֵינוּ יהוה אֶחַד)

Hear Yisrael YHVH is our God,

YHVH is one.

The concept of loving God requires a total and complete commitment to His cause and His word. A denial of that, according to Jesus' words, is an "unworthy of me" situation. Jesus knew that conflicts would come and devotion would be strained, because of family, society, and other interests.

Following him requires some self-denial and establishment of priorities. Peter had forgotten those things Jesus taught, and found himself in a state of denial in Matthew 26:75, and experienced bitter failure and weeping.

Sometimes humility only comes when one finds themselves powerless and failing.

The teaching of Jesus about denying self and accepting the will of God, seems so far away when faced with the threat of torture or death. Counting the cost of discipleship presents a stark reality when the powers that be, begin to threaten life and limb.

Mark 8:35 mentions about saving one's life, and losing one's life, and Jesus stresses the way to save one's life is to go all out for him and his **good tidings** message. He then equates it with gaining the whole world or losing the <u>soul</u> (Mark 8:37-38). It's noticeable that in verse 35, the Greek Manuscript word "life" was begotten from the term ψυχη and the word "soul" also comes from the same source (#5590, Strong's Concordance).

Since Jesus used the word "deny," relative to himself (***deny me***), and as pertains to self-denial practiced by his followers; we should take a quick notice of the Greek manuscript word behind the English form <u>deny</u>, and see exactly how a concordance defines the term.

That form is απαρνεομαι (*#533 apar-ne'om-ahee*), meaning; to *deny utterly, disown, abstain.* In the writings of Paul, he refers to denial of the carnal nature, and explains it to be the lust of the flesh, which one should not yield himself unto.

In truth we need to grasp that all the confidence levels of followers of Jesus, are to be accepted and believed because of his teachings. But it must be emphasized there are numerous warnings in the words of Jesus, which tend to de-emphasize the human ego factor.

Scriptural principles were given by Jesus and self-abasement is opposed to self-exaltation. An old saying used to exist among my teen friends, who in those days were hopeful leaders and lovers of God. The saying was similar to some of the sayings of Jesus: *the way up is down, and the way down is up.* We understood it to be a call to humbleness and abandonment of self in order to ensure success in spiritual matters.

Jesus gave a similar saying when teaching his immediate followers in Matthew 23:11-12, "But he that is greatest among you shall be your servant. And whosoever shall exalt himself shall be humbled; and he that shall humble himself shall be exalted."

The underlined terms "exalt himself" are

contrasted with <u>humbled</u> and are supported by desire to be great, rather than to be a humble servant. *It all depends on which inner urge we yield ourselves unto.* It's within our power to "deny ourselves" or to "exalt oneself." The very next verse (23:12), shows the power of taking the humble path by saying: ***"And whosoever shall exalt himself shall be abased; and he that shall humble himself shall be exalted."***

To abase oneself is the proper way to behave since our faith has been placed in one greater than ourselves. Jesus went so far as to tell us what would happen in the event we should decide to exalt ourselves; we would be abased.

It's quite a change for us, since we have learned how hard and demanding it can be, to make a living in a world that requires excellence and sophistication at every level. Only those who have the driving force to sit atop the heap, have a greater chance in this age of expertise. This is what we have observed and geared up for in a carnal dog eat dog arena. But the Kingdom of God is not that way at all.

The disciples of Jesus has wondered "who" would sit at Jesus side in the literal kingdom, and had even argued of which one it would be. In one biblical example, even the mother had requested favor for her sons.

Matthew 20:20, "Then came to him the mother of Zebedee's children with her sons, worshipping him, and desiring a certain thing of him (20:21) And he said unto her, What do you want? She said unto him, Grant that these my two sons may sit, the one on your right hand, and the other on the left, in your kingdom."

Of course Mother's want their children to be at the top of the class or the teacher's pet, but in matters pertaining to heaven, the ultimate decision belongs to God. However, that wasn't only a mother's desire, the sons in this example were fussing about a position at the top. The next selection of verses show what I refer to.

Let us look at another verse in Mark 9:33. "And he came to Capernaum: and being in the house he asked them, What was it that you disputed among yourselves by the way? (34) But they held their peace: for by the way they had disputed among themselves, who should be the greatest. (35) And he sat down, and called the twelve, and said unto them, If any man desire to be first, the same shall be last of all, and servant of all."

Jesus had been on the mountain with Peter, James, and John, and came down after Moses and Elijah had appeared with him there. The other disciples were left below the mountaintop, and were asked to cast out a demon. They failed to cast out a dumb spirit, but the father of the boy came to Jesus begging help, and Jesus cured the boy.

As they continued in the way walking, the disciples were disputing about power positions or perhaps who could have cast out the spirit, if only they had been there. Jesus quickly assessed the dispute, and dealt with the matter, including the "desire" to be dominant.

On this occasion as well as others already mentioned, Jesus talked about leadership character and humility. Christians are not supposed to be in a "contest" for power, authority, or popularity.

The New Testament gives many guidelines for behavior among leaders and followers, as I will soon show in this writing, but I want to show for the moment, that under the law, one man was excellent in "humility."

His name was Moses. Our keyword for locating the search criteria about Moses and

Christians Are Not Supposed To Be In A "Contest" For Power, Authority, Or Popularity.

others in scripture who were humble is the biblical word **_meek_**. Numbers 12:3, **_"Now the man Moses was very meek, above all the men which were upon the face of the earth_**."

It is unlikely that Moses was just naturally a man of mild disposition, since he rose up and defended a fellow Hebrew who was being abused by an Egyptian in the account given in Exodus 2:11-12. As the account relates, Moses slew the Egyptian and hid his body in the sand.

Being an authority figure and raised by the princess of Egypt, Moses must have had a sense of privilege and authority about himself, in order to interfere in a slave and master incident. On the next day he tried to interfere between 2 Hebrews in their controversy, and recognized that it was known about his killing of the Egyptian the day before. It appears that Moses had a temper problem, rather than a humble or meek disposition. Had he learned about being authoritative and proud in demeanor in the Egyptian courts? *Had an inner sense of being chosen, caused him to become hasty in his decisions?*

We see the same traits of quick response in the matter of the daughters of Midian in Exodus 2:17, when Moses stood up against the shepherds who wouldn't allow the women to water their flock. *Women's rights were defended long ago by a man who fled Egypt.* I suspect the problem Moses had was not being "meek," rather it was an anger issue combined with authority driven leadership skills.

But in the process of leading Israel out of Egypt, due to his encounter at the burning bush, he began a humbling experience under the mighty hand of God.

As a fugitive from Egypt, rather than a prince in the king's court, he was experiencing a huge demotion from worldly power and authority. But he was learning to do the bidding of the Master of the universe, and that on the job training would teach him the importance of allowing the Lord God to be in control of all the authority matters.

Jewish tradition as well as scripture shows how that Moses' character was fine tuned to such an extent, that he was able to write Numbers 12:3, at God's command. Who would dare write about himself the words: ***the man Moses was very meek***? Only an egotist, or an extremely obedient and meek person. In my thinking, I can just see and hear Moses, saying as God dictates; *Write this. Moses was probably saying: Who? Me? Uh, uh, not me. Again the Lord says: You are My scribe; write.*

When people have a quick response attitude and finally learn that some things can only be accomplished by the Lord God, the learning curve is achieved. I don't think it took long at all for Moses to realize that a prince of Egypt was totally powerless, when he encountered the angel at the burning bush. Uh, huh, okay Lord, if you say write; I can do that.

Leadership demands are huge when millions of people are involved, and the Lord knows exactly how to shape and prepare His servants for duty. I am going to give some more verses from the bible written below, so as to be able to grasp in a condensed form, what the importance of a "meek" attitude may be.

Psalm 22:26 The meek shall eat and be satisfied: they shall praise YHVH that seek him: your heart shall live forever.

Psalm 25:9   The meek will he guide in judgment: and the **meek** will he teach His way.

Psalm 37:11 But **the meek** shall inherit the earth; and shall delight themselves in the abundance of peace.

Psalm 76:9 When God arose to judgment, to save all **the meek** of the earth. Selah.

Psalm 147:6 YHVH lifts up **the meek**: he

casts the wicked down to the ground.

Psalm 149:4 For YHVH takes pleasure in His people: He will beautify **the meek** with salvation.

Isaiah 11:4   But with righteousness shall He judge the poor, and reprove with equity for **the meek** of the earth: and He shall smite the earth with the rod of His mouth, and with the breath of His lips shall He slay the wicked.

Isaiah 29:19 The meek also shall increase their joy in YHVH , and the poor among men shall rejoice in the Holy One of Israel.

Isaiah 61:1   The Spirit of YHVH GOD is upon me; because YHVH has anointed me to preach good tidings unto **the meek**; He hath sent me to bind up the brokenhearted, to proclaim liberty to the captives, and the opening of the prison to them that are bound;

Amos 2:7 They pant after the dust of the earth on the head of the poor, and turn aside the way of **the meek**: (partial citation).

Zephaniah 2:3 Seek you YHVH, all you **meek** of the earth, which have wrought His judgment; seek righteousness, seek meekness: it may be you shall be hid in the day of the anger of YHVH.

Matthew 5:5 Blessed are **the meek**: for they shall inherit the earth.

Matthew 11:29 Take my yoke upon you, and learn of me; for I am **meek and lowly** in heart: and you shall find rest unto your souls.

Matthew 21:5 Tell you the daughter of Zion, Behold, your King comes unto you, **meek**, and sitting upon an ass, and a colt the foal of an ass.

1 Peter 3:4 But let it be the hidden man of the heart, in that which is not corruptible, even the **ornament of a meek and quiet spirit**, which is in the sight of God of great price.

My summary shows that there are 12 Old Testament verses with the word **meek** in them, and 4 New Testament verses with **meek** in them. Thus, our total is 16 King James Version verses, with that particular word.

The Hebrew manuscript form for the English **meek** is:

עָנָו

Strong's Concordance #6035; *meaning; humble, meek, poor.*

The Greek Old Testament translation form in

the Septuagint is πραυς #4239, and this same Greek form is the one written in New Testament manuscript. Theological dictionaries also define it as mildness of disposition, gentleness of spirit.

We have pointed out the use of the word meek as related to Moses, and given verses to show its use in Old Testament writings, as well as some teachings of Jesus about the kingdom concept, as given by gospel authors.

These principles also apply in other New Testament writings, as I shall write for our readers in this next chapter.

Biblical Humility

PART 2

English translation words in our bibles give us numerous ways to express words like *meek, humble, abased,* or even words like *submitting,* all of which link to the Hebrew and Greek manuscript forms. When one does a computer based search program of the bible, the discoveries are almost endless. It's pretty easy to find volumes of information in a matter of split seconds, that would otherwise take much longer and require many scholars to complete. I try always to do as much research as possible from the scriptures, on any given subject.

Doctrines of the past must pass the test of information gathering, that was never possible a hundred years ago. Space age technology based on facts rather than theory, has caused so much progress and advancement in society, and history.

Our main trouble may be in the fact that it takes long periods of time for detailed information to filter down to the common people, since truth is not always accepted as fact among the common and traditionally oriented people.

I'm talking about matters of faith as related to scripture. For those who love God, we trust his writings to always be true, even when we don't understand all that is written. But in these days and times, we can look into and examine bible verses as no one has ever done before.

Our findings at times have a tendency to upset a traditional view, and for all of this we are left to wonder just how accurate some of our theology truly is. I have observed this over and over. Case in point;

What took the Church world so long to break away from the dogma of "works" alone, and other traditions of a universal Church?

Didn't one Martin Luther protest in 1517 AD, about 95 matters in play amidst the believers in the organized church? How many years is that from 33 AD and the outpouring of the Holy Spirit? That involves a period of 1,484 years from the outpouring of the Spirit till Martin's revelation.

What took the church so long to come to that realization? It seems that the so called protest was not really effective, or else the church community has allowed itself to be deceived.

Now here we are in 2016 AD, and seeking to discover out true foundations. Yet the same type forces still exercise control and domination over and among millions of people in organized Christianity. They are yet under the doctrines and authority of Jezebel-Nicolas types, or non-spiritual church groups.

It really does require that we be meek and humble, rather than stand on the shoulders of those who went before us, and tried their best, working with tools of inadequate nature to expound the scriptures. My constant and daily study of scripture discovers that many things are not accurately aligned to texts. But I have

Our Findings At Times
Have A Tendency To
Upset A Traditional View,
And For All Of This
We Are Left To Wonder
Just How Accurate Some
Of Our Theology Truly Is.

refused to allow it to hinder or destroy my faith, although I have developed phrases like "intellectual dishonesty" to describe what I know to be errors, by folks who knew better than to tamper with scripture by inserting words and phrases not consistent with manuscripts.

I have written a book entitled *Truth Nuggets* which shows deviations from manuscript texts. It's really quite simple, but it indicates various deviations. With that in mind, let's approach what the New Testament writers wrote about meekness, or humility. I have chosen to use the phrase "yourselves" because of its personal impact.

Jesus had used the concept of abasing oneself, and we find the author of the Book of Jacob (James) 4:10, saying: ***"Humble yourselves in the sight of the Lord, and He shall lift you up."***

The previous verse had emphasized a humbled state of mourning, weeping, and heaviness, as opposed to laughter and joy. Jacob has asked them to ***"submit yourselves unto God, and draw nigh unto Him."*** He had further said: ***"God resists the proud, but gives grace unto the humble*** (James 4:9)."

The terms *proud, humble, submit, mourn, weep,* and *heaviness* are all found in the stretch of verses between James 4:6 and 4:10. God wants His children to be lifted up, and encouraged, but it is the result of knowing His Christ, rather than the uplifting of one's own self.

God makes "grace" available to those who humble themselves in His Presence. A very similar writing is found in First Peter 5:5-6, which teaches younger members in the church to be submissive to elders who are setting an example.

"Likewise, you younger, submit yourselves unto the elder. Yes, all of you be subject to one another, and be clothed with humility: for God resists the proud, and gives grace to the humble. Humble yourselves therefore under the mighty hand of God."

The verse also teaches subjection to one another. Being obedient to one another, and being obedient to God, is not so difficult to obtain, since the command to be clothed with humility is as though without it, one is stark naked in the sight of God. *This notion of being clothed with humility, relates to a fastening or girding one's self, with a humble opinion or a modest demeanor.* Elsewhere in the New Testament, we are told to **not think of ourselves more highly than we ought to think but to think soberly, as God has**

dealt to every man the measure of faith
(Romans 12:3).

It's needful to look at the term "resisteth" since it was written by Peter that God treats proud persons with "resistance." That Greek manuscript term is Strong's #498, αντιτασσομαι *an-tee-tas' som-ahee*, or to *range in battle against; oppose oneself.* Proud people have a war to fight; it's a war "against God."

This subject of humility is strongly associated with the inner self, as indicated in New Testament verses I was able to locate. Since Jesus had used the terms meek, lowly in heart, and abased, in reference to people and a kingdom attitude, I thought that the term "yourselves" would be an excellent choice for examination. It fits nicely into the subject matter with quite a few New Testament references.

Each of the verses used here relates directly to meekness and New Testament instruction or commands given by apostolic authority, to behave or act in a Christian manner.

Acts 2:40 exhorts, *to save yourselves*

Acts 15:29 wrote, *keep yourselves*

Romans 6:13 ~ *yield yourselves* unto God

1 Corinthians 7:5 ~ *give yourselves* to fasting, prayer

1 Corinthians 11:13 ~ *judge in yourselves*

2 Corinthians 13:5 ~ *examine yourselves*

Ephesians 5:19 ~ *speak to yourselves* in psalms/hymns

Ephesians 5:21 ~ *submit yourselves*

James 4:7 ~ *submit yourselves* to God

James 4:10 ~ *humble yourselves* in the sight of...

1 Peter 4:1 ~ *arm yourselves likewise* (as Jesus)

1 John 5:21 ~ *keep yourselves* from idols

Jude 21 ~ *keep yourselves* in the love of God.

This collection of sayings from the New Testament in the Christian Bible, indicates a constant necessity of self-discipline and self-examination in order to continue in spiritual growth and maturity.

Even when the Christ has saved us and dwells within by his Spirit, some constant effort is required to stay spiritual. It's sort of like keeping house; if you fail to do it, you'll soon have a mess. To assume that no human effort is required in the plan of salvation, is exactly what the adversary wishes for one to assume.

For this reason and many others, God requires a humble person, to dwell within, as written in the ancient prophets;

"Who shall abide in your Tabernacle and dwell on your Holy hill? He that walks uprightly and works righteousness, and speaks the truth in his heart." (Psalm 15:1-2).

This can only be, because the believer has submitted to the Almighty, and has chosen to yield his will unto the service of the Master. *Maybe we have failed to consistently follow the example set by Jesus, as a humble and righteous servant of the Most High God.*

We will take a look at the humbleness or meekness of Jesus, as written by the author of the Book of Hebrews, but before we begin that examination, I want to refer once again to a few more examples of pride and haughtiness, as noted when reading some Old Testament verses.

My first verse selection is from Proverbs 16:18: saying; "Pride goes before destruction, and an haughty spirit before a fall."

Now the book called by the English name "Proverbs" is actually a Book of Parables; it contains the wisdom of Solomon and his father king David, as was given by the Lord. The very next verse stresses "a humble spirit" (Vs. 19).

Jesus was not the first person to teach by parables, rather we find them employed by Balaam, Job, Samson, Solomon and others in scripture. It is written in 1 Kings 4:32; that Solomon's parables (proverbs) were 3,000 and his songs were 1,005. They were used as a teaching tool, and a means of instruction for Jewish children, according to the writings of Proverbs 1:1 - *the parables of Solomon the son of David, king of Israel*.

The teaching method is easily noted in the English wording of the Book of Proverbs, which says in 23 verses, *my son*. We found that the parables were said to be from Solomon in Proverbs 10:1, and Proverbs 31:1 wrote, that *king Lemuel* received them as a *prophecy that his mother taught him*.

The mother is not named by the text, and we should consider that Proverbs 1:1 clearly mentions some parables as being from Solomon, son of David, king of Israel. Whether or not Solomon wrote all of those in the Book of Proverbs, may be difficult to answer, since *Agur* is named in Proverbs 30:1, as having "words" relative to parables (Proverbs).

Some Jewish traditions mention that *Agur* is one of Solomon's many names. Also, other Jewish sources identify Lemuel as Solomon, taking advice from his mother Bathsheba, but there is no clear evidence of this (Wikipedia source). One writing describes 7 names for the man Solomon, based on Hebrew writings and texts: **Solomon, Ithiel, Jakeh, Jedidiah, Kohelet, Agur,** and **Lemuel**.

Varying opinions and scholarship about the true source of the Book of Proverbs, do not take into account many variables such as Gentile writers and converts to Judaism, whose words were worthy of being used to promote wise and capable thought processes, and the ability of wise Jews inspired by God, who could take account of truths and implement them into the teaching structure of Judaism. This is exactly what David did in the Book of Psalms, for sages say that he rewrote many Psalms using the words of Moses and others, to complete those writings, and was able to do so by the Holy Spirit upon him.

One thing is certain, the words and sayings in the Book of Parables teach about many moral facets of life, and show how that pride, haughtiness, and lack of humility leads to a path of destruction. At times, and within a religious community, a mind set or attitude, is developed due to a holiness aspect, which is taught strongly by leaders of that particular group.

In separating from sin and worldliness, a superior attitude is developed by its adherents. This can be a dangerous thing, since outsiders don't feel welcome in such an atmosphere, and the potential for conversion is greatly reduced.

In ancient Israel, some had developed a false sense of trust and security, because of their righteous behavior. The prophets cried out against such haughty attitudes. Notice Isaiah 3:16 - "***Moreover YHVH says, because the daughters of Zion are haughty, and walk with stretched forth necks and wanton eyes, walking and mincing as they go, and making a tinkling with their feet: Therefore YHVH will smite with a scab the crown of the head of the daughters of Zion, and the YHVH will discover their secret parts***."

These daughters of Zion are mentioned as wealthy, proud, and arrogant women of Jerusalem by some Jewish commentators. They had dominated and ruled over the nation. Isaiah foretold what would befall them in the verses that follow. Others say, that these women appeared tall and walked with erect posture to attract attention. Another said of them; that public life was corrupted by leaders and family life was undermined by those women, instead of teaching moral values in the home, they were concerned with gratifying their own selfish desires. They had become pampered and spoiled, and developed a passionate love for luxurious dress and finery.

Other comments were made by commentators which imagined them to wink at younger men as they walked, with painted eyes and makeup, and beckon to the younger men. They were said to walk with affixed bells on their shoes that would jingle as they walked, inviting the attention of young men.

Each of the different Jewish commentators which I read after, described the demeanor as haughty. Sadly, I have noted similar behavior at times in public church services. I don't really know if it's a matter of overdress, immodest dress, or attention getting, or imitation of a star struck mentality like an entertainer might display. But why would we need to wear glittering clothes, or glittering eyes into the House of prayer? Why would a young lady wear a see through blouse or a low cut dress to the House of God? Why would any man want to come to the House of prayer in a muscle shirt with hundreds of people present?

It seems to me that some Christians have

accepted the "me" concept, rather than the "thou" concept. I truly hope that I am wrong about opinions based on observation made over the years. Whatever the case may be, we can only hope that immodest behavior and lack of respect for the God of the House of God, will be corrected by a healthy dose of the fear of the Lord.

I also found some verses in Isaiah 2:11-12, concerning Judah and Jerusalem saying;

"The lofty looks of man shall be humbled, and the haughtiness of men shall be bowed down, and YHVH alone shall be exalted in that day. For the day of YHVH the Lord of Hosts shall be upon every one that is proud and lofty, and upon every one that is lifted up; and he shall be brought low."

That prophecy continues to impact inanimate things in the next verses; high cedars, oaks, hills and mountains, fenced walls, towers, ships, and the loftiness of man. The symbolism of "high" things is contrasted with the "exaltation" of the Lord alone (Isaiah 2:17).

In Hebrew Bible scriptures (Old Testament), **the day of the Lord** (YHVH), is an awesome and horrific time for non-repentant mankind.

In the Christian bible (New Testament), we

find wonderful examples of the humility of Jesus, and I think it best to show how he lived it out, since we have cited various examples of what he taught his disciples and the crowds that followed him.

Our Example

Of a Humble Man

PART 3

Our New Testament uses the word example for some behavior patterns to imitate. Jesus himself did acts of humility to demonstrate that we should also practice certain behavior in regard to humility as discussed earlier from John 13:15. His words were; ***"you should do as I have done to you"*** (role of servant to master).

Paul wrote to his son in the faith in 1 Timothy 4:12, "You be an example of the believers, in word, in behavior, in love, in spirit, in faith, in purity."

That's great advice for every believer, as well to be passed from adoptive father to a son of the flesh. Apostle Jacob (James) also used the same fatherly words, saying; *"Take, my brethren, the prophets, who have spoken in the name of the Lord, for an example of suffering affliction, and of patience."* (Jacob 5:10).

Apostle Peter then points to Jesus in 1 Peter 2:21- "For even hereunto were you called, because Christ also suffered for us, leaving us an example, that you should follow his steps."

Jesus suffered for us, and the example of his life, leaves a pattern that is necessary for us to follow when called upon to do so. However it requires a humbled state of mind, to realize that *the sufferings of this life are not worthy to be compared, to the glory that is to be revealed in our behalf.* (See Romans 8:18).

In the Epistle to the Philippians 2:3, Paul had written about lowliness of mind, which enables one to realize his role in this world for the sake of the kingdom of God:

"Let nothing be done through strife or vain glory; but in lowliness of mind let each esteem other better than themselves."

Wow! How does that fit into the psychobabble which we hear spouted today from a few pulpits? It doesn't seem to help my ego a bit. All I have been hearing for the last 25 years or better is that I need to have a better self-image. I need to become more positive and have better self-esteem. I, I, I, me, me, me, ooops. What did he say? **Lowliness of mind**! Other better than self? I can never be a winner? *Awww*; that's not right, is it? Mocking humor intended.

Grasping a humble mind set is not easy if you've been pampered and coddled all your life, and told that you can be the "greatest." Then when you get everything you want all the time, and that pattern is not continued; what next? Every person can't be president at once.

Knowing that Jesus is our pattern or example for humility, we look for verses from the New Testament which give information about his moral character and demeanor. I especially favor Philippians 2:8, *"**And being found in fashion as a man, he humbled himself and became obedient unto death, even the death of the cross**."*

The very words, *he humbled himself*, indicates a personal choice and willingness to do the will of the Father in the heavens. Jesus had a will of his own, as does every normal human being, and any concept of being Jesus Christ a "superstar" was not his purpose in life. The Satan had offered him all the "world" and its kingdoms in Matthew 4:8-9, but Jesus would not bow down and worship the Satan, nor would he allow ego worship in any measure. Neither did Jesus allow the Satan to provoke him into tempting fate, by casting himself down in expectation of supernatural and angelic rescue (see Matthew 4:6).

Nor would he submit himself to Satan's suggestion that he turn stones into bread to satisfy his hunger after 40 days of fasting in Matthew 4:2. Jesus was sent to perform a mission, and nothing could detour him from the heavenly mandate of obedience unto death.

The insight of the author of Hebrews 2:9, captures the heavenly mandate and Divine mission, saying; "But we see Jesus, who was made a little lower than the angels for the suffering of death, crowned with glory and honor; that he by the grace of God should taste death for every man."

His purpose for being born as a human, was that he might experience death on behalf of all sinning humans. If He was a member of the Trinity before he was "made" a human, there is no other reason for he to have become a man. Only his death and resurrection could atone for all sins and sinners.

Being made lower than angels (Hebrews 2:7), made flesh (John 1:14), made Lord and Christ

(Acts 2:36), made to be sin (2 Corinthians 5:21), made of a woman, made under the law (Galatians 4:4), made of no reputation, and made in the likeness of men: (Philippians 2:7); are all characteristics of every human being in the lowliest sense. The only exception could be in the sense that other humans are NOT Lord or the Christ. But we must make allowance for language differences and nuances of word meanings that have developed over periods of time, and due to spiritual developments.

For instance: the Greek term *kurios*, meaning, Lord or master, is applicable to any landowner or sir, but not so in the case of YHVH (the Divine name), for only He is reverend and Holy. But in Jesus' case the Greek term *kurios* takes on a new meaning. Likewise the term *christ*, χριστος from the Hebrew, was also written of <u>David</u>, <u>Cyrus</u>, and the <u>tabernacle priests</u> in ancient Israel, in the Greek translation of the Hebrew text, made around 200-300 years before Jesus came to earth. Even the translation term rendered "<u>false christs</u>" in Matthew 24:5, and coming from the mouth of Jesus, indicates deception and does no honor to the term "christ."

Rightly dividing the word of truth is only possible for those who constantly study what God has written and caused to be written. Others are subjected to being misled unless they are under the care of the Holy Spirit and the chief shepherd. God given pastors will teach that which is approved by the Holy Spirit which guards and calls to memory the words of Jesus.

All the examples I have given below with the word "**made**" are in six verses using different Greek forms as follows:

John 1:14 Strong's #1096, γινομαι, *to become, come into existence*, (English= **made**).

Acts 2:36 Strong's Concordance #4160, ποιεω, *make, produce* (English = **God has made**).

2 Corinthians 5:21 Strong's Concordance #4160 ποιεω, *make, produce*, (English=**He has made him**).

Philippians 2:7 Strong's Concordance #2758, κενοω, *to empty*, (English = **made himself**).

Hebrews 2:7 and Hebrews 2:9 Strong's Concordance #1642, ελλαττοω, *to make less or inferior*, (English translation = **Thou madest him** vs, 7, and **made a little lower** -vs. 9)

Galatians 4:4 Strong's Concordance #1096, γινομαι same as John 1:14, "*to become, come into existence,* (**was made flesh** and was, **made of a woman**).

Hebrews 6:20 Strong's Concordance #1096, γινομαι same as John 1:14 and Galatians 4:4, *to become, come into existence* (our English translation term was **made an high priest**).

Every reference with the word ***made*** in that verse group, relates to the fleshly body of the man Jesus.

The New Testament relates to Jesus before his incarnation, as αλφα – ομεγα (A–Ω), which in English would be *First and Last, or beginning and end.*

This is explained by Greek language students, as the first and last letter of the Greek alphabet.

A similar comment is made in the Old Testament regarding the God of Israel, in three verses of Isaiah 41:4, 43:10, and Isaiah 44:6. In 43:10 the Hebrew reads thus:

רִאשׁ֔וֹן וְאֵ֥ת אַחֲרֹנִ֖ים

first and last

The Hebrew manuscript of Isaiah 43:10 wrote these words:

$$\text{(לְפָנַי לֹא־נוֹצַר אֵל וְאַחֲרַי לֹא יִהְיֶה)}$$

Before Me no God was formed and after Me none will be.

Our third verse of similarity is Isaiah 44:6, which was written:

I am First and I am last, and beside Me there is not a God.

These next few verses show a pattern of humility about Jesus as a son of God, during different stages of his life. But before he was "made" or came into being as a man, he was not formed or made by any power or being, for beside him there was no other.

"Who in the days of his flesh, when he had offered up prayers and supplications with strong crying and tears unto him that was <u>able to save him</u> from death, and was heard in that he feared" (Hebrews 5:7).

This verse above shows the man Jesus to be a person of prayer, and a person with strong crying and tears with his supplications. It also relates that his prayers were answered, and that the fear of God controlled his behavior.

The very next verse in Hebrews 5:8, expresses a wonderful relationship between Jesus the man, and his heavenly Father, saying; *"**Though he were a Son, yet learned he obedience by the things which he suffered**."*

The word <u>obedience</u> indicates that Jesus was compliant and submissive to the will of the Heavenly Father, and that his obedience and humility caused him some suffering. Yet it was written of him: *"**being made perfect, he became the author of eternal salvation unto all them that obey him.**"* Obedience was a learned discipline among humans, and not just an automatic by product of human birth.

Jesus, as a youth, was perfectly compliant to his earthly mother, and his adoptive father, as we will now show from writings in Luke 2:41-51.

"Now his parents went to Jerusalem every year at the feast of the Passover. And when he was twelve years old, they went up to Jerusalem after the regulation of the feast."

This verse shows that Jesus had a family life, and was involved in the religious aspects of their worship and faith. According to Jewish tradition, Jesus would participate in the yearly Passover celebration as commanded by Moses in Exodus 12:24.

"And when they had fulfilled the obligation, as they returned, the child Jesus tarried behind in Jerusalem; and Joseph and his mother knew not of it. But they, supposing him to have been in the company, went a day's journey; and they sought him among their family and acquaintance. And when they found him not, they turned back again to Jerusalem, seeking him."

Family groups must have journeyed together to attend the feast of Passover, as indicated by the translation terms in <u>the company</u>.

This was probably due to security and safety issues. The group must have been large since the 12 year old Jesus wasn't noticed to be missing for a day's journey. His parents had "supposed" him to be present, but it soon was realized that he was missing.

"And it came to pass, that after three days they found him in the temple, sitting in the midst of the doctors, both hearing them, and asking them questions. And all that heard him were astonished at his understanding and answers. And when they saw him, they were amazed: and his mother said unto him, Son, why have you thus dealt with us? behold, your father and I have sought you sorrowing. And he said unto them, How is it that you sought me? know you not that I must be about my Father's business?"

His parents were no longer operating in the realm of supposition, after they found Jesus, but they had to seek for 3 days among the crowds to find him.

This event provides good preaching material for Christians and religionists who practice their faith, but go along and leave Jesus behind. What a lesson! His mother Mary, had said to him after locating Jesus in the Temple; "*your father and I have sought you sorrowing*."

Perhaps that statement "thy father," struck a chord in Jesus' heart; for he replied, "*I must be about my Father's business*." His staying behind, had a Divine purpose that only he as a 12 year old boy could comprehend at the moment. His contact with the religious teachers of Judaism in his Father's house, caused amazement among teachers because of his questions and answers.

"And they understood not the saying which

he spoke unto them. And he went down with them, and came to Nazareth, and was subject unto them: but his mother kept all these sayings in her heart."

The wording of that verse in Luke, relates how keenly he understood about the House of God, and the leadership role of teachers of Judaism. His zeal for God's House had overwhelmed him, and in spite of his spiritual elation, he at the same time realized the sorrow of his mother and adoptive father, and went down to Nazareth with them, **and was subject unto them**.

What tremendous humility for a 12 year old boy that could amaze elders and yet humble himself to his poor parents. Intelligent children can recognize both spiritual matters, and matters related to authority and respect for all. Such was the 12 year old boy, Jesus. During his youthful years he was an example of humility and subjection to authority.

The writer of Hebrews 12:2, accurately captures the role of Jesus, and his devotion and attitude toward the mission given him by God, and uses it as an example for the believer, saying: **"Looking unto Jesus the author and finisher of faith; who for the joy that was set before him endured the cross, despising the shame, and is set down at** *the right hand of God.*"

His humble attitude and devotion to the God given mission was what produced joy in his life. Jesus was able to experience joy because he carried out the Father's plan.

Most of us find satisfaction in our own efforts and achievements, but Jesus found joy in doing the Father's will, as though it were meat or food, giving energy to continue through the ordeal.

That was also the Jewish way, to take joy in fulfilling a command given by YHVH (the LORD).

Among the most devout of Orthodox Jews, many males take great joy in being able to fulfill even one command given by God.

The ultra-devout, among orthodox, are called *charedim,*

(חֲרֵדִים

tremblers; mentioned in the Hebrew text of Isaiah 66:5.

The concept of trembling at the word of God, relates an attitude of reverence for what God is speaking or what he has said in the past. Some who assume that they are super spiritual have lost a sense of fear and reverence for God, and feel that they are so advanced in Christ, that they have bypassed such a negative concept as **fear**.

Have they forgotten that humility is the balance in spiritual matters? In the Jewish tradition it has been taught with words like this: **Think not that He is your friend; lest you forget that He is your king**.

It has a tendency to bring a more sober attitude to a person who may have moved beyond the fear factor. *Reverence for God is shown by reverence for His words*. This is probably one of the reasons why the Orthodox Jewish male wears a *kippah* (or yarmulke) on his head: to show that he is under the authority of one higher than himself.

In past times the head covering or skullcap was worn when at synagogue or reading and studying the scripture, but that has changed somewhat. It's a voluntary matter for the most part for the male since there is no bible verse requiring such action.

In my opinion it is a sober and serious recognition of the voluntary submission of oneself to a higher authority.

In the Christian bible (New Testament), Paul's teaches in his writings to the Corinthian church, that a man when praying or prophesying should not have his head covered, for in doing so, he dishonors his head (Christ).

See 1 Corinthians 11:4. He also gives rules for married women in Corinth, which are no longer followed in most churches today.

*Jesus Was Able To
Experience Joy
Because He Carried Out
The Father's Plan.*

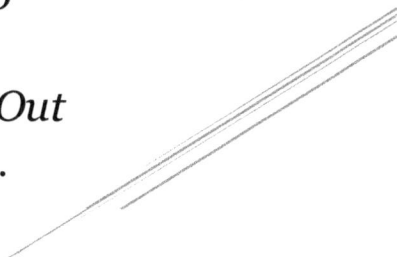

Sobriety

PART 4

My computer based biblical search results examining the words **sober, soberly, soberness and sobriety**, gathered a total of 17 verses with those 4 English New Testament forms. Since they connect so well with the Christian humility theme, we should examine them. I listed them below in order, as displayed in my bible search computer findings.

When we think of being "sober," in our English culture, it often has to do with not being inebriated or drunken. God only knows how much tragedy has been caused in this world by intoxication and people partaking in strong drink. These days it seems more and more that drinking alcoholic beverages has involved the youth and children of the church and Christian families. That's sad. It often has started with social drinking, and then escalates to experimenting with forms of alcohol used, and to partying among teens or college students. It almost always leads to trying different drug usage beside alcohol. In America millions have been killed on our highways, and hundreds of thousands injured over the years due to drinking alcohol while driving an automobile. The bible warns about drunkenness and its effects. But I can't tell you how many times I have heard alcoholics say; "I can quit any time I want to."

But they never seem to want to quit, and the next thing I know; they are dead. I have seen many times in families what drunkenness has done, and have had some familiarization with it among my relatives. I use those words to show how that a sober minded concept is important in every walk of life. If we desire to be at our best, then we must have good judgment and sensible logic. This also applies in spiritual matters, as we shall see in the New Testament verses I have assembled below.

Paul's letter in Second Corinthians 5:13 writes: "For whether we be beside ourselves, it is to God: or whether we <u>be</u> <u>sober</u>, it is for your cause."

Our Greek Manuscript term is (#4993, *sofroneh'o*, σωφρονεω, and means of *sound mind*. A sound mind with good judgment is important when teaching others, or when receiving the teachings of God. It is inseparable from any concept of Christian humility.

"Therefore let's not sleep, as do others; but let's watch and be sober." 1 Thessalonians 5:6

In this verse example, the Greek word for sober is # 3525, *nay'fo*, νηφω, meaning; abstain from wine, or figuratively, *be discreet*. Paul had in the previous verses, wrote of the day of the Lord coming as a thief in the night, and reminded them, that people are sleeping at night, but Christians are children of light and watchful, and not as the drunken who imbibe during the night.

"But let us, who are of the day, be sober, putting on the breastplate of faith and love; and for an helmet, the hope of salvation." 1 Thessalonians 5:8 –

This Greek term is the same as above, Strong's Concordance #3525, νηφω. The next example with the term "sober" is in the letter to the young pastor in 1 Timothy 3:2- "**A bishop then must be blameless, the husband of one wife, vigilant, <u>sober</u>, of good behavior, given to hospitality, apt to teach**" #4998 *sof-'rone*, σωφρων, meaning; *safe, sound in mind.*

These leadership qualifications for a "bishop" are extreme, and what one would expect for an overseer or superintendent. But Paul's list of qualifications are NOT observed by numerous churches of today, since some pastors or overseers have been married more than once.

Paul also stresses about a sober behavior pattern for the preachers wife, saying in 1 Timothy 3:11 - *"**Even so must their wives be grave, not slanderers, <u>sober</u>, faithful in all things**"* (Strong's #3524, *nayfal'eh os*, νηφαλεος, figuratively, circumspect, sober). The qualifications; *grave, not a slanderer, and faithful* are what is expected for the wife of a man of God.

In the letter to Titus 1:8, Paul further expresses qualification for a bishop, writing the following: *"**But a lover of hospitality, a lover of good men, <u>sober</u>, just, holy, temperate**"* Our Greek word for "sober" here is Strong's #4998 *so'frone*, σωφρων, safe (sound) in mind. This person is generous to guests, and fond of being generous to them, as well as observant of the law, and having good control over his emotions. Paul elaborates further in Titus2:2 - *"**That the aged men be <u>sober</u>, grave, temperate, sound in faith, in charity, in patience**"* (#3524 *nayfal'eh os*, νηφαλεος).

70

According to Paul's epistle in Titus 2:4, the aged women are to be teachers of good things to the younger women: *That they may teach the young women to be sober, to love their husbands, to love their children*. Our Strong's Concordance number is # 4994, *sofronid'zo*, σωφρονιζω; *to make of sound mind*. Christian humility requires some instruction, and submission in behalf of sober thinking and actions.

It may be somewhat of a surprise, but even the young men were given sobering counsel in Paul's letter in Titus 2:6, saying; "*young men likewise exhort to be sober minded*." This injunction is very difficult for young Christians (young men) to accept.

But it is not only apostle Paul who gave such serious instructions. Notice the words of apostle Peter in First Peter 1:13 - "Wherefore gird up the loins of your mind, be sober, and hope to the end for the grace that is to be brought unto you at the revelation of Jesus Christ" (Strong's #3525, νηφω).

Girding the loins of one's mind, is like putting on a belt to hold up the loose trousers, lest when walking or running, they fall, and trip you tangling the feet and causing a fall.

Peter also puts the reason for the instruction

for being sober, in perspective by relating it to an end time scenario in 1 Peter 4:7- *"**But the end of all things is at hand: be you therefore sober, and watch unto prayer**"* (#4993, *sofroneh'o,* σωφρονεω). He also relates it in 1 Peter 5:8, as follows: *"**Be sober, be vigilant; because your adversary the devil, as a roaring lion, walks about, seeking whom he may devour**"* (# 3525 *nay'fo,* νηφω, same as 1 Peter 1:13).

Although Jesus has conquered death and the devil in our behalf, we need to be wise in our logic and recognize that the wicked one is yet an active force, to try and defeat humanity by deception. That can be noted in reading the book of Job, in which the Satan tries always to interfere with the earthly sons of God by tempting them to fail. He uses affliction and trials to tempt humans to be discouraged and lose faith in the Almighty one.

The apostle Paul used the term soberly in Romans 12:3, writing: "For I say, through the grace given unto me, to every man that is among you, not to think of himself more highly than he ought to think; but to think soberly, according as God hath dealt to every man the measure of faith" (Strong's #5426 froneh'o, φρονεω, to exercise the mind).

When words such as those come from the

lips and mind of one as learned as Paul was, we do well to heed them. It seems that Christians in America today have such a generous amount of self-esteem, that the injunction to not think so highly of one's self is such a negative one. Our faith movements and media personalities, seem to refute the sober attitude with nearly all that they proclaim. Perhaps they have more wisdom and faith than apostle Paul. It may be with them, that they are unable to condescend to men of low estate, for the grace of God has enabled them to rise higher spiritually than all men. Have they forgotten what the grace of God teaches?

A quick reading of Titus 2:12 might cure such illness;

"For the grace of God that brings salvation has appeared to all men, teaching us that, denying ungodliness and worldly lusts, we should live <u>soberly</u>, righteously, and godly, in this present world"

(#4996, *sofron'oce,* σωφρονως, = *sound mind*).

The constant and repetitious media presentation of "grace" and grace alone as a means of salvation, consistently ignores the words given in that verse written by the great apostle.

He wrote and told his followers exactly what

grace teaches, but the grace and grace alone presentation, removes personal responsibility from every believer and lays it all on the actions of God, while taking away the free will or choice of humans. It's a dangerous viewpoint since it conflicts with all the teachings or actual words of Jesus as recorded by gospel authors. Words like *strive, seek, beware, watch, pray, don't faint,* etc., etc. It indicates that they think their doctrine and preaching excels the very words of Jesus.

It is not good when the words of Jesus do not have priority, as they did over the life of apostles like Peter and Paul. In Acts 26:25 Paul wrote: **"But he said, I am not mad, most noble Festus; but speak forth the words of truth and <u>soberness</u>"** (Strong's Concordance #4997 *sofrosoo'nay,* σωφροσυνη).

The concept of Christian humility affects not only our mental viewpoint and consequent behavior, but it even regulates our style of dress in a world going astray with flamboyancy and enticing demeanor, as noted by unrestrained clothing styles. I'm talking about a lack of modesty, and not just cultural differences in dress.

It had begun to be a problem in the church world in Paul's day, and he warned about it in a letter to pastor Timothy, in First Timothy 2:9 -

"In like manner also, that women adorn themselves in modest apparel, with shamefacedness and <u>sobriety</u>; not with braided hair, or gold, or pearls, or costly array" (**#4997**, *sofrosoo'nay*, σωφροσυνη, = soundness of mind*).

Such words nowadays are considered *nit picking*, if used in church meetings. That's a taboo subject for nearly every pastor who wants a congregation of any size. Few pastors in America would dare to minister on such a subject, while following the words and writings of Paul. Yet when it comes to the message of saving grace, they prefer to accept the words of Paul above the words of Jesus. They do not wish to be called a clothes line preacher, or hobby horse rider. They think that preachers and apostles should not be talking about apparel, because it has nothing to do with souls and salvation.

Provocative dress among congregant's is not a subject that fits into the sermon schedule, nor is the subject of modesty among men and women. And what is modest apparel? Our Greek parent word (manuscript) is κοσμιος (Strong's number 2887, *kos'mee-os*, meaning; *well arranged, seemly*).

How do the words shamefacedness, braided hair, gold, pearls, and costly array relate to the

Greek manuscript writing, and our English translation terms? Rather than translate them, I will show Strong's concordance numbers and listed Greek meanings.

First one is this old type English translation word *shamefacedness*. Our Strong's Concordance word is αιδως, #127, *ahee-'dos*, meaning; *a sense of shame, honor, bashfulness, downcast eyes*. Wow! The next phrase in our verse was braided hair, from the concordance number 4117, πλεγμα, *pleg' ma*, meaning; *woven, twisted, plaited, web.*

Lastly, we should look at the terms *costly array*, from the Greek being assured that it relates to expensive clothing, as is easily determined by the terms being included with words such as *gold* and *silver*. Thus, shamefacedness, or a bashful countenance, matches the arrangement of a holy woman as described by the apostle.

It is important to understand by those words, that both the home, and the Christian assembly not be a place where immodesty or lack of holiness are constantly manifest. This is further expressed in First Timothy 2:15, regarding Christian husbands and wives. **"Notwithstanding she shall be saved in childbearing, if they continue in faith and charity and holiness with sobriety"**

(Strong's #4997 *sofrosoo'nay*, σωφροσυνη, = *soundness of mind, sanity, self-control*).

This verse shows the importance of husband and wife behaving (they), in a faithful way of holiness, charity, and a sound mind. In so doing, a wife is promised to be spared (saved) in childbearing. The Greek form for "saved" is σωζω, #4982, having meanings such as, *heal, preserve, safe, deliver*.

Being able to understand all these nuances regarding the concept of Christian humility, is in itself a matter of willingness to allow the grace of God to grant self-control.

If we are unwilling to humble ourselves under the hand of God, no amount of grace can save us.

The movement of God in this world, the kingdom of God, is not a robotic spell cast upon a believer as a spell from above. It's a kingdom ruled by God, but it is comprised of those who choose to pursue Him.

He as a gentleman, never forces allegiance upon His subjects, and that in itself indicates his great attributes. One of which is humility. Amen.

He As A Gentleman,
Never Forces Allegiance
Upon His Subjects...
And That
In Itself Indicates
His Great Attributes.
One Of Which Is Humility.

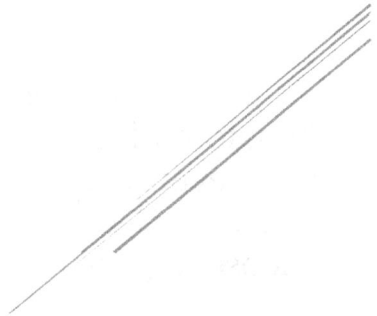

Attitudes: Law, Grace

And Gospel

PART 5

The evolution of Christian doctrine of today, is based mostly on the teachings of Paul, as outlined in letters to the churches he founded. Those instructions and teachings seem quite different than what Jesus himself actually taught, as described in the Gospel accounts. Most church groups place emphasis on Paul's words as a means of salvation, rather than focusing on the written words of Jesus.

This is evident in the doctrines about "grace" and "love," as an effortless means of human redemption in the scheme of God's plan. But, did Jesus actually teach that human effort was not necessary in the plan of salvation? We recognize that "human response" to the word from God, has always been a serious factor of consideration relative to man's salvation. It's quite evident in the Genesis account, since the Lord God had spoken to the "man," and given him one negative command, after having told him what he "could" do, in regard to the Garden of Eden and its many trees. A concept of permission and non-permission was developed at the creation of humankind. ***"Of every tree of the garden you may freely eat: But of the tree of the knowledge of good and evil, you shalt not eat of it"*** (Genesis 2:16-17).

The concept of obedience toward a word which God had spoken, is developed at the onset of humanity. A Divine principle of "obedience to God's word" is given only after the Lord had specified that which was allowed. The consequences for disobeying what God had spoken were outlined in the same word of God; ***for in the day that you eat thereof you shall surely die.*** It was the Lord God who first spoke of negative consequences for the disobedient human.

We do well to remember that to eat, and not to eat, were "commands" given by the

יְהוָה אֱלֹהִים

(Lord God).

In this case a word of God was actually described as a "command" of God, and combined both a positive and negative injunction.

Such description is important to recall, since the Masoretic Hebrew text names the command of the Lord God as:

וַיְצַו יְהוָה אֱלֹהִים

and the Greek Septuagint Version wrote; *the Lord God gave a charge to Adam.*

Our Greek root word from the Septuagint version is λεγων, and it is associated with the Greek term known as "logos," which Christian bibles and scholars link to Jesus, the "word of God" (see Greek manuscripts of John's Gospel, chapter one).

When he came to this world, in human form, exactly what did Jesus say to a person in Luke 13:23, who had asked along with others in the crowd: **Lord, are their few that be saved?**

A concept of "being saved," may be linked to the scriptural assertion that Adam and Eve were driven out of the Garden of Eden, because of the "sin of disobedience" as mentioned in Genesis 3:23-24. Paradise was lost, and the way of the tree of life must be preserved so that "sinners" could not eat and live forever.

But, in later Jewish thinking, for the most part, they were covenant people because they kept the commands or words given by God to His people, and were not worried about not "being saved." God had instituted "covenant" with them when they had agreed to hear and obey His words from Sinai as written in Exodus 19:8 – "*And all the people answered together, and said, all that the Lord has spoken we will do.*" The matter is further sealed in Exodus 20:19, when the people also said; "*Speak you with us, and we will hear: but let not God speak with us, lest we die.*"

Fear from God had fallen upon them because of the thundering, lightning's, and the trumpet sound, with the mountain smoking. But they would accept Moses and his teachings as from God, and they were yet willing to obey and serve God under the leadership of the prophet Moses. They had heard the thunderous voice of God, and became fearful, yet they would obey His words. *Just let Moses speak;* they said.

In the verse mentioned in Luke 13:23, a question arose about "few being saved," although it seemed non Jewish; Jesus answered with specifics in Luke 13:24, saying; "*Strive to enter in at the strait gate: for many, I say unto you, will seek to enter in, and shall not be able.*" Our Greek manuscript word is σωζω (sode-zo), Strong's Lexicon number 4952), and was rendered into the English form "saved." More completely defined by the words; *save, keep safe and sound, to rescue from danger and destruction.* Safety and salvation are indeed an act of God, in many instances, but "to strive" is an action required by humans.

A key word is the English "strive," coming from a Greek word αγωνιζωμαι (Strong's # 75), which has similar sounds as the English "agonize." Listed meaning in the Greek Lexicon are; *to enter a contest, contend in the games, contend with an adversary, to struggle.*

According to Luke 13:26-27, Jesus describes the "non-strivers" as **workers of iniquity**, who knock on the masters door, saying; **Lord, Lord, open to us**. His reply was to them: **I know you not whence you are.** They had involved themselves in behavior inconsistent with the masters will, nor had they struggled or "strived" to enter in at the **strait gate**.

This example in Luke chapter 13, about persons striving to enter the strait gate, doesn't relate well to the message about a believer being justified by "faith alone." The view of Jesus, and from his own lips, is quite consistent with the letter of Apostle Jacob (James), to the church and twelve tribes scattered abroad, regarding *faith without works is dead, being alone* (Jacob 2:17). His comment about faith in Jacob 2:14, also says; "*though a man say he hath faith, and have not works? can faith save him*?" Apostle Jacob appears to be exactly on the same page as Jesus in that matter of "saving faith."

Abraham's faith was proven in the matter of the "test" in Genesis 22:1. But, Abraham's faith was justified and proven to be true, in that he proved to himself that His love for God, surpassed his love for the son that God had provided for him, in spite of the deadness of Sarah's womb. That point is also written about by Apostle Jacob, who stated in Jacob 2:21, saying; "*Was not Abraham our father justified by works, when he had offered Isaac his son on the altar*?"

In the plan of grace and mercy, some sort of human effort is always necessary, whether it be repentance, or an action of exercising the human will to be in position to receive God's benefits. Jesus had told his apostles in Luke 24:47-48; "*Repentance and remission of sins should be preached in his name among all nations beginning at Jerusalem. And ye are witnesses of these things*."

In the beginning of the Christian Gospel, after Jesus' resurrection, his command was to preach repentance and remission of sin in his name among all nations. When has that command been changed and by whom?

Does repentance require a human effort? Does it require an exercise of the human will? The notion or concept of effortless faith, does not appear even to fit into the overall scheme of the writings or letters of Paul, as shown among the churches.

As a matter of fact, the same Greek root word (Strong's 375), which was rendered "strive" in Luke 13:24, was used by Paul in his letter to the Romans 15:30. It was written there, "***strive together with me in your prayers to God for me***." Paul asks and even pleads to the Romans, to "strive together" in prayer for him. This request requires much human effort in regard to "prayer." It requires that all in the Roman church to whom his epistle is addressed, that a concerted prayer effort be made in his behalf.

In another epistle written by Paul to Timothy, he uses a word similar to our English term "athlete." We read that if a ***man also strive for masteries, yet is he not crowned except he strive lawfully***. That word in Strong's Lexicon, #118, is used in referral to an athlete who grapples or contends for the wreath or the crown. Even the early church was supposed to "contend" for the faith, which was once delivered to the saints (Jude 3). Again, the word similar to "agonize" in sounding, was rendered "earnestly contend." Who says, that under the terms of the gospel of grace, no effort is required, except to believe?

The power of human choice is within itself an effort to choose the good path. rather than the evil or disobedient way. Automatic salvation is not granted to those who are non-seekers of the kingdom of God. Didn't Jesus say in Matthew 6:33- "***Seek ye first the kingdom of God and His righteousness***" An aspect known as "seeking" is the human contribution to God's Divine plan of redemption. Jesus paid the penalty for mankind sins, but humans must choose to accept the benefit. When human effort is belittled in regard to God's grace and mercy, then the so called "gospel" becomes perverted, because it is a robotic spell from God, rather than a matter of free will.

Words from the lips of the master have been ignored to some extent, by those who wish to simplify or make a universal appeal to the nations.

But what did Jesus actually say in regard to the Heavenly Father and His will? Did he not say in Matthew 7:21 – "**He that <u>does the will</u> of my Father shall enter into the kingdom**?" Some effort is involved in "doing" God's will. Then he further mentions in Matthew 7:24 – "**those who hear these sayings of mine and <u>do them</u>, is as a wise man who <u>builds</u> his house upon a rock**." In Matthew 7:26, only the foolish man <u>builds</u> upon the sand. I have purposely underlined all the meaningful verbs or action words for emphasis. Doing and building are easily understood by all.

Automatic Salvation Is Not Granted To Those Who Are Non-Seekers Of The Kingdom Of God.

Just because Jesus took our penalty of death, which every sinner deserved, as stated by the Lord God in Genesis 2:17, and the prophet Ezekiel in his words written in Ezekiel 18:4, the believer is not free to continue to flagrantly walk in sins and disobedience. We have been destined to be **blameless and harmless the sons of God without rebuke, in the midst of a crooked and perverse nation, among whom you shine as lights in the world**" (Philippians 2:15).

In each believer, it is required to **work out your own salvation with fear and trembling** (Phil. 2:12). This particular word "work" in that verse of Philippians. means to *work fully, accomplish fully, finish, fashion, deed, perform, work* (Strong's Greek #2716).

One translation uses the word "cultivate." At any rate, salvation not only requires deliverance by the Lord, and His grace, but depends on human effort of work, deed, and performance of the will of God.

Only works and deeds prove the genuineness of faith after one is converted. As written by Apostle Jacob even the **demons believe and tremble** knowing about the One God, but demons do not perform works or deeds of righteousness (James 2:24). Humans are justified by faith with "works," and not by faith alone.

Paul's arguments about being saved by faith without the works of the law, seems to me to be redundant, since he wrote in Romans 3:20, **"Therefore by the deeds of the law shall no flesh be justified in His sight."** Yet he again wrote in Romans 2:13 – **"but the doers of the law shall be justified."** Is he failing to take into account in his logical arguments, that doers of the law who believe and act upon God's word, the law, are just like father Abraham who was willing to take his only son for an "olah" on a mount of which God would show him? If the law of the Lord is the word of God, then what is the problem?

The words of Jesus in Matthew 7:12, show a huge difference between Paul's opinion of the law, and what Jesus clearly stated: "***Therefore all things whatsoever ye would that men should do to you, do ye so to them: <u>for this is the law and the prophets</u>***." Jesus' view certainly expresses accuracy about God's love and grace under the law and the prophets. He knew that the Heavenly Father was generous under the law, and that God was willing under the law and prophets to give "good gifts" to all who asked His assistance.

That precise viewpoint about the law and prophets, expressed a correct attitude about the purity and love of God, as shown in the writings of the law and the prophets. The writings of the prophets of God, were given mostly by command and vision from the Lord, and they were the spoken and written WORD OF GOD. To say that the "law" was not the word of God, would be utter blasphemy.

It is possible that Paul's contact with religious Jews had blinded his vision, and introduced hypocrisy or bias into his own life, because of all the additions made to the law, by

Jews of that period. After his encounter with Yeshua (Jesus) on the Damascus road, he saw the need to become a Christian, and repented of his murderous ways, and hateful intent. His persecuting ways were somewhat self-deceptive, since his self-assessment was that he "*profited in the Jews' religion above many my equals, how that beyond measure I persecuted the church of God and wasted it*" (Galatians 1:14).

His zeal for Jewish religion, was superior, but seemed to lack a sense of focus for the true substance of the law and prophets, since he allowed himself to "waste" the church, which at that time consisted mostly of fellow Jews. Such madness drove him to break some laws of scripture in the Old Testament, where Moses has written; "*You shalt not avenge, nor bear any grudge against the children of your people, but you shall love your neighbor as yourself*" (Leviticus 19:18).

A Jew was required under the writings of Moses, to have trial and witnesses, before any actions such as death penalty could be instituted. Those who study the writings of Moses, know that many details are involved and penalties prescribed for every departure from that faith; yet both Paul and the high priest who gave him letters to harass Christians, seem quite guilty of hypocrisy in those matters.

The 19th chapter of Leviticus is certainly "law," but in that chapter Moses commands the children of Israel to love thy friend, love thy people, love thy brother, and even to love or respect the stranger, who travels in the midst of Jews.

The Hebrew words are several which indicate that love is high "respect" for

אֲמִיתֶךָ , אָחִיךָ , הַגֵּר רֵעֶךָ ,)

which literally means; your friend, the stranger, your brother, your people.

Those words are given under the law of God and Moses, and show reverence and respect for rights of others in ancient times. Jesus knew all this, and spoke highly of the law and the prophets. Most of us do not recognize that "love" is "respectful" of the rights and consideration for others. We have been duped into thinking that love is only an emotion or a romantic inclination.

Jesus had told his followers in Matthew 23:2: "The scribes and Pharisees sit in Moses' seat: All therefore whatsoever they bid you observe, that observe and do; but do not you after their works; for they say, and do not. For they bind heavy burdens and grievous to be borne, and lay them on men's shoulders; but they themselves will not move them with one of their fingers."

Jesus was quite aware of the hypocrisy of certain Jewish leaders, but he did not condemn the whole legal system known as the law of Moses, rather he encouraged people to respect the entire system as had been set up by the word of God. After all, "sitting in Moses' seat" was the highest honor that any human could ever attain, since it was written of him: "*And there arose not a prophet since in Israel like unto Moses, whom YHVH knew face to face, in all the signs and wonders which the YHVH sent him to do in the land of Egypt to Pharaoh, and to all his servants, and to all his land*" (Deuteronomy 34:10-11).

An explanation of the verse is given by the word of the Lord to Miriam and Aaron in Numbers 12:6-7 - "Hear now My words: If there be a prophet among you, I YHVH will make Myself known unto him in a vision, and will speak unto him in a dream. My servant Moses is not so, who is faithful in all My house. With him will I speak mouth to mouth, even apparently, and not in dark speeches; and the similitude of the YHVH shall he behold: wherefore then were you not afraid to speak against My servant Moses?"

The relationship between God and Moses was so great, that God became angry when Miriam and Moses spoke in some way against Moses, because of his marriage to the Ethiopian woman.

The lawgiver whom God had chosen and revealed Himself to in such a unique way, was not dependent on dreams and visions, or trances. God could speak to him plainly, and face to face. The words which he gave to Israel, God's treasured and holy people, were given according to the "voice of God," as written in Deuteronomy 30:10, which wrote: ***"you shall listen to the <u>voice of YHVH your God</u>, to keep His commandments and His statutes which are written in <u>this book of the Law</u>."***

Such verses are ample evidence to illustrate that the "law" was expressed by the voice of God, and that the Old Testament was not only known as the "law," but was the written word of God in a book form.

It didn't seem too difficult for ancient Israel to grasp and perform, since the true Israelite believer was told in the words of Moses: ***"For this commandment which I command you this day, it is not hidden from you, neither is it far off. It is not in heaven that thou should say, who shall go up for us to heaven, and bring it unto us, that*** *we may hear it and do it? Neither is it beyond the sea, that you should say, Who shall go over the sea for us, and bring it unto us, that we may hear it and do it? But the word is very near you, and in your heart, that you may do it.*"

These verses show that under the law, it was not considered difficult or impossible to perform or DO what the Lord commanded.

Blessings were abundantly promised to those who made the effort to hear and to do. It's quite obvious that only a believer would act, and do, after hearing that word.

The law contained a huge amount of spiritual information, and its writings or book of the law, was described by Jesus in Luke 24:44, as being divided into 3 sections, which he called *the law of Moses, the prophets*, and *the Psalms*. In Luke 24:25, he even mildly rebuked his disciples by saying; "*O fools, and slow of heart to believe all that the prophets have spoken*." Luke also wrote in Luke 24:45; "*Then opened he their understanding, that they might understand the scriptures.*"

Jesus named the law of Moses, the writings of the prophets, as the scriptures. Luke also narrates his gospel in 24:47 in this manner;

"*And beginning at Moses and all the prophets, he expounded to them in all the scriptures the things concerning himself.*" It's next to impossible to defend Paul's attitude and writings against the law, when you actually read what Jesus said about those scriptures.

His arguments against the law, should be understood as arguments against hypocrisy within the organized system understood or known as the law. His master Jesus always denounced hypocrisy and hypocrites, but never disdained or demeaned the law of God and Moses.

The disciples walking with Jesus in Luke 24:32, after his resurrection, are reported to have said: "*He talked with us by the way, while he opened to us the scriptures (law).*" During this time period, and immediately after his resurrection, no New Testament verses existed, thus, to assert that in that setting "scripture" is reference to any New Testament verses is without logical or written proof. Jesus' only bible was the Old Testament. At that time, no New Covenant terms had yet been written.

Jesus himself had not written any documents, nor had his immediate followers taken upon themselves to "write" of his words, events, or details of the story about him. After the great commission to spread the good news after his resurrection, he sent his apostles to bear the tidings to the nations. At this point, the efforts to spread the word by various writings and languages, as well as word of mouth, began to flourish and take root.

An explanation that New Testament writings were also scripture, began to take hold among the disciples and followers of Jesus. Until then, the only testimony of God was the things which He wrote and caused to be written, and some were contained in the Ark of the Covenant, of which is recorded in heaven, as declared by Revelation 15:5. Others were recorded in book form. Thus, the "commandments of God" and the "testimony of Jesus Christ" are a theme in the Book of Revelation 12:17.

Arguments have been set forth by certain followers of Jesus, that all his instructions were given <u>before</u> his actual passion, death, and resurrection. Therefore they conclude that Paul's instructions in the New Testament are based on inspiration that came as a result of the event of the cross and death of Jesus. Such persons conclude that we are under a plan of grace and the law is no longer valid. That flies in the face of scripture which clearly asserts in Hebrews 1:2, that Jesus was the <u>last day</u> spokesman in God's behalf. – *"[God] has in these last days spoken unto by his Son, whom He has appointed heir of all things*." Are we still in the last days?

That verse suggests that since the times of the prophets past, we have entered into an event specific period, known as "last days," and it is traced back to the coming of the "Son," who is God's last day spokesman. Thus, to assert that the words of Jesus, though delivered under the law period, are no longer binding because of the cross, are absolutely heretical.

Didn't he say, "*heaven and earth shall pass away, but my words shall not pass away*" (Matthew 24:35)? The final spokesman for the last days is Jesus. Not me, not you, not Paul, not Peter, but Jesus. No words should outweigh the words of Jesus for a Christian. It was Jesus who commanded the post resurrection apostles to **teach all the things which I have taught you among the nations** (Matthew 28:20). *Teaching them to observe all things whatsoever which I have commanded you*, was possible to be done by those who were witnesses to three and one half years of personal hands on ministry with Jesus.

The argument used and based on John 1:17, is not valid - **the law was given by Moses, but grace and truth came by Jesus Christ**. The same verse that emphasizes "grace" emphasizes truth. Thus, we know that all that Jesus said is <u>truth</u>. God's spokesman cannot lie, and his teaching is supposed to be the foundation of all things, even before and after his death, burial, and resurrection. He did nothing to demean or deny the law, or negate any word of God.

Any so called plan of salvation which nullifies the teaching of Jesus, even if disguised by terms such as love and grace, must be considered biblically illogical and in error. Grace was always evident under the law and before the law. Even in a Gentile world, Noah found grace with God. His efforts and works were not the saving action of God, but his efforts and works were a result of his faith in the one who can save, rescue, and deliver.

When preaching a gospel of faith minus works for salvation in Christ, it is hardly ever heard what Paul actually taught regarding grace and what it teaches. Notice Titus 2:11-12:

"For the <u>grace</u> of God that brings salvation has appeared to all men, <u>teaching</u> us that, <u>denying ungodliness</u> and <u>worldly lusts</u>, we should live soberly, righteously, and godly, in this present world."

The same apostle who mouthed faith without works, is in this epistle to Titus emphasizing that "grace" teaches something to all whom experience salvation.

What does grace teach? *It teaches a sober and responsible life style which does not defy the word of God in any way.* It teaches humility and purity, as well as separation from ungodliness and worldly lusts. Grace also teaches us that we are God's treasured people and we should be zealous of good works. Any message or sermon supposed to be from God, does not contradict a notion of personal responsibility toward God, nor is it devoid of holiness, that is scripturally defined.

It seems so odd to me, that many preachers and teachers use Paul's epistles or letters which he sent to churches he founded, as a means of presenting a salvation message. But when it comes to pastoral epistles and letters, with oodles and bookoos of instruction, they refuse to use those words and views for doctrinal instructions. Wow! We could elaborate about so many things, but suffice it to say that Paul's words about married women who speak out, and fail to gain the hubby's permission, would flat destroy many groups, causing schism nearly everywhere.

Many church groups which take the words of Paul to promote doctrinal positions or beliefs, would suddenly be split wide, when confronted with his letters showing the teaching about women, speaking out in services without permission of their husbands, was declared as a **commandment from the Lord** in First Corinthians 14:34-35. It's expressed again by him in 1st Corinthians 14:37. Paul even uses the force of the Law of Moses, to support his claim to **keep silence**.

Now that Christians, for the most part in America have a complete bible in every home, we can no longer sustain a claim for ignorance as an excuse to ignore what is written in Christian letters to churches. If we don't believe what Paul said is for us, let's just admit that we can't agree with him, or with the law about obedience and submission which God spoke to Adam and Eve at the beginning. But, when we keep insisting that we believe the whole word of God, it seems to me that our position is quite hypocritical.

That same logic raises its head again and again, when we hear preachers and teachers constantly demeaning the law of God and Moses, in order to show that the message of love and grace is superior to what God spoke to Moses, Elijah, and Jesus. Do they think that God finally discovered mercy and grace, when Jesus came into this world? Any careful student of the Hebrew scriptures which we call the Old Testament, can show the lovingkindness of the Lord, again and again in the biblical account.

Grace and favor has always been available for converts and strangers, who wished to be a part of the family of God. When Israel left Egypt, a <u>mixed multitude</u> attached themselves to Israel, and left Egypt with them. An action of favor.

The notion of law keeping was necessary at times, to maintain order among groups numbering as much as a million or two. Yet our teaching about the law, seems at times quite biased and unfair. Even after the resurrection of Jesus, the apostles and elders at Jerusalem, sent letters to the church groups telling them to ***<u>keep the decrees</u> that were ordained*** by themselves (Acts 16:4).

That word **decrees** needs some clarification from Strong's Concordance #1378, its manuscript form is δογμα, listed as follows: doctrine, decree, ordinance; or decree of the Roman Senate, rules, requirements of the law of Moses; carrying a suggestion of severity and threatened judgment, or decree of the apostles relevant to right living.

They had just dealt with matters about Gentile converts being required to keep the Jewish laws, and concluding that only a few things were required of new Christians (Acts 15). Now they turn around, and write letters to Gentile converts to Jesus, and giving *<u>commandments of the Holy Ghost</u>* for them to keep (Acts 15:28). Wow! *Extreme caution should be used when conflicting in any way. with the words of Moses and Jesus, or Holy Ghost commands and apostolic decrees.*

Acts 21:25 reminds Gentile converts to Jesus, **keep themselves from idols and things sacrificed to them, from blood, and sexual sins** (fornication, etc.). Some action is required by believers to "keep themselves." Even Paul the apostle wrote to Christian converts in 1 Corinthians 5:11, "**<u>not to keep company</u>, if any man that is called a brother be a fornicator, or covetous, or an idolator, or a railer, or a drunkard, or an extortioner; with such an one not to eat.**"

Paul is making new rules for his converts to keep. Maybe he thinks that those rules will keep Christians from being drawn back into paganism by way of association. His words make it certain that He is only relating to one who professes Christ, but whose life does not reflect a drastic change from past sin. He doesn't want shame and disgrace to be brought to the Christian believers community. But, effortless grace will not make it happen; it requires some rules, counsel, and instruction. In 2 Timothy 5:22, Paul writes to Timothy, "**keep yourself pure**."

It takes more than effortless grace to pass the test of temptation. Purity comes to those who choose to "keep themselves." Paul also writes saying; *"fight the good fight of faith."* How does one fight without grappling? The manuscript reading in 1 Timothy 6:14, uses word soundings similar to our English word **agonize** and **agony**, for the terms **fight**.

Grace and love of God, delivered us from sin, but effort, struggle, **and sometimes agony**, is needed to keep us in the faith. The apostle Jacob (called James), wrote in Jacob 1:27: *"to keep himself unspotted from the world."* To write such words shows that human effort is needful, for the *kosmos* (worldly order) can produce blemishes on a believer. Always remember how the Lord God created light and darkness, then He separated the light from the darkness for the sake of humans. He also divided the land from the water in various ways. We have to learn so separate ourselves somewhat from the darkness and bad influences.

It's never wrong to separate or sanctify ourselves to God, and separate ourselves from evil of the world. The word sanctify means to set apart unto God. Sometimes separation is necessary to maintain a holy communication with Him. But, let's not allow ourselves to become haughty, proud, or self-righteous, for that also brings blemishes into our lives or character.

The mighty Samson only failed after he began to relinquish his vows of abstinence, and all the things his parents had taught him from a child. In spite of it all, the Lord God used him to bring hope to Israel and dread to the Philistines. We should maintain a healthy respect for the laws of God and Moses, while embracing the faith in Jesus. This is also displayed in wording of 1 John 2:3. ***"We know that we know Him, if we keep His commandments."***

If New Testament writings and letters are His commandments, then let's give reverence to them. If the law of God and Moses have been nailed to the tree, let's remember that no prophet in Israel ever saw, as did Moses according to Deuteronomy 34:10-12. So, if our theology exceeds what Moses proclaimed as God's word, we had better be prepared to say, that we also have a face to face, and lip to lip relationship with God. That means we don't need dreams, visions, trances or revelations.

Further still, as Christian Gentiles we were not told by New Testament writings to keep the Jewish laws, but since the law was the word of God, neither were we given authority to demean, negate, or loosen the Jewish scriptures from the force of the word of God to them. There is no place to stand for those who make void the law of God and Moses, for numerous time in scripture it was written,

(בְּרִית עוֹלָם)

everlasting covenant.

Christians also, were given rules for right living. Likewise, 1 John 3:23, **"*we keep His commandments and <u>do</u> those things that are pleasing in His sight*."**

It's our privilege to <u>do those things that are pleasing in His sight</u>. Just as Jesus always did those things pleasing in God's sight, we emulate the teacher and seek always to please Him. Matthew 3:17 says of Jesus, **"*And lo a voice from heaven, saying, This is My beloved Son in whom I am well pleased*."**

Some have suggested that in the Church world there is no law but love. That is not altogether true, but we must remember that all efforts and actions must be done with a loving or charitable intent (1 Corinthians chapter 13).

It is also clear according to 1 John 5:2- "By this we know that we love the children of God, when we love God, and keep His commandments. For this is the love of God, that we keep His commandments: and His commandments are not grievous."

If one refuses to honor or reverence the love of God, who sent His Son into the world, and negates all his words as non-binding, then how are we to understand that they follow Jesus, who never one time negated the writings and commandments of Old Testament prophets?

According to the Christian Bible, as outlined in the Book of Revelation 14:12: "Here is the patience and faith of the saints: here are they that keep the commandments of God, and the faith of Jesus."

That comment is said by some, that this pertains to the non-rapture group, which faces the great worldwide <u>pressure</u> (θλιπσις translated tribulation), and those who become believers during that period.

For their sake, and the sake of those who constantly negate the words of the law, I point out a verse in Revelation 22:9 ***"for I am thy fellow servant, and of thy brethren the prophets, <u>and of them which keep the sayings of this book</u>: worship God."***

Our previous verse in Revelation 22:8 identifies that the person talking to John the Revelator <u>is an angel</u>. But, this same angel is <u>a fellow servant</u>, <u>a prophet</u>, as well as a <u>raptured believer</u>, **and of them that keep the saying of this book**. Hmmm! A raptured, and pre tribulation believer, who <u>keeps the sayings</u> of this book.

New Testament writings seem in some cases to be ignored by some modern media Christian preachers, who assert with great plainness and boldness, that <u>righteousness</u> requires no effort except faith in Jesus. The same messengers also promote that personal <u>holiness</u> almost comes by accident due to a believers faith.

If perhaps they are exactly right, what then is the purpose of the abundance of epistles and writings about such things regarding behavior and moral conduct for Christians? Why should earliest preachers and teachers spend so much time with quill and inkwell to instruct new believers?

When salvation is free for believers, because Jesus suffered the death penalty for every sinner, there seems to be no personal responsibility for ones conduct. Words like, **strive**, **labor**, **agonize the agony** (fight the good fight of faith), **seek**, **knock**, and **build**, are all action words which require some sort of human effort.

There is no one time knockout punch, or faith that removes effort or personal trust on a daily basis in the battle against sin, and the carnal nature of the flesh. If the Apostle of God said: ***I die daily***; what was his problem? Isn't he supposed to be beyond struggling, as some of his supposed followers, have espoused?

A belief that produces action and activity due to faith in God, is exactly what Jesus taught. As he spoke and said, which others wrote: ***"let your light so shine before men that they may see your good works, and glorify your Father which is in heaven."***

WHAT DOES GRACE TEACH?

It Teaches A Sober And Responsible Life Style Which Does Not Defy The Word Of God In Any Way.

It Teaches Humility And Purity, As Well As Separation From Ungodliness And Worldly Lusts.

Grace Also Teaches Us That We Are God's Treasured People And We Should Be Zealous Of Good Works.

The Trend Of Lawlessness

PART 6

It's not hard to see that the world is full of constant struggle to achieve, whether for the better or for the worse, depending on the attitude of the human heart. Some seek to improve many things because of oppression or mistreatment. Others may have legitimate grievances due to injustice or violent activity. I always wonder why God said; **"the heathen rage and the people imagine a vain thing"** (Psalm 2:1).

Sometimes the rage of people leads to violence, in the streets, even before facts of grievance can be determined. In other situations, the rage of the heathen in times past, and in the book of Psalms, is indicated to be because of the Divine appointment and God's designated rule. David the Psalmist also foresaw that some people rebelled against God's choice, and tried to break away from the bands and cords of authority (Psalm 2:3).

In modern times people with a grievance take to the streets more than ever, hoping to gain attention for their perceived injuries. This happens because of all the media attention allotted to bad news, and the breaking news story needing a "scoop." Good news just doesn't get attention, because it's the normal, and nobody wants such mundane reporting. Oh, but the excitement of bad news, gets attention. Many times protests in the streets which involve authority figures, and the populace, leads to rioting and anarchy. This happens in countries where permissive attitudes toward protest exist.

Thank God for freedom. But when freedom leads to riot and destruction, this is harmful to any nation. But why should this happen in a Christian country, where freedom for all exists?

Obviously freedom is not freedom when hearts are evil and bias is deeply embedded in hearts of the citizens. There must be inner change in hearts and minds before society can improve itself and take advantage of its freedom to move up to a higher level.

Crime, criminals, and lawlessness, must be controlled by authority figures, since those who have chosen bad behavior, cannot be rewarded by complacent justice. It matters not whether injustice is served up by authority figures, courts, policemen, or crooks on the streets. It must be fairly and even handedly dealt with. Lady Justice is supposed to be blindfolded.

But I see a great need among Christian groups as well as political ones and society itself. It is the need for respect and lawful behavior among all groups. It should have begun long ago, beginning with the church assemblies of this, and all nations.

It has to do with a "lawless" attitude, and the church itself must bear a great burden of responsibility in that regard. The pulpit may be guilty by way of complicity, <u>simply due to silence</u> or ignorance of the actual teachings of Jesus.

Segments of the church of the past and of today, have excelled in presenting a message of salvation, "without the works of the law." Pulpit messengers and evangelists have rang out a gospel of grace and grace alone.

It has been said thousands and hundreds of thousands of time, **we are not under the law,**

but under grace. The equal opportunity was stressed so that whosoever will may come and be saved. That in itself was so good. An anti-law viewpoint because of the New Testament writings, was grasped by bible readers, promoted by preachers and teachers, and has begun to bleed through into the whole of society. It has always been so and may continue until the millennium, but in the times of lawlessness, street violence, rape, burning, looting, and murder; how shall we of the church not frame our words more carefully in regard to the "law?"

Our Old Testament word for "law" is the Hebrew form תּוֹרָה (torah), and it is found in 18 Old Testament verses as יְהוה.

תּוֹרָת

(toraht YHVH) Law of the LORD.

The phrase means law, direction, or instruction. Our Greek Septuagint form νομω κυριου , and is the same Greek form as found in 3 New Testament verses (Luke 2:23, 2:24, and Luke 2:39). So, we find 21 English verses with exact manuscript forms agreeing in Greek Old Testament and Greek New Testament terminology. My computer searching phrase was in English, the "**law of the Lord**."

Going one step further, I searched on the terms **law of God**, to make sure the same word "torah" was included in both of the Divine names (YHVH and Elohim). It was so. I found 7 verses which wrote exact English terms "**law of God**." Seven verses were found in the Hebrew Old Testament, and three in the Greek New Testament.

When we look at the Greek Septuagint and see how they translated from the Hebrew, we find the terms νομου του θεου and νομον του θεου in all 7 verses, from the Greek standpoint. This establishes strong links from Greek Old to Greek New Testament, made around 300 years before Jesus' day (See Joshua 24:26, Nehemiah 8:8, Nehemiah 8:18, and Nehemiah 10:28).

Our other 3 verse are references to Paul's personal observance of the law, after having become a Christian. We have already shown that the Greek New Testament and Greek Old Testament term for "law of the Lord" and "law of God" is *nomos*, and that the parent word was the Hebrew term (*torah*) for the mentioned verses. Now what is enlightening for us, is the fact that Paul the apostle says about the law of the Lord, or the law of God, when he is not defending himself or his Christian followers from so called

Judaisers; He <u>delights</u> in the law. Let's write Romans 7:22 below.

"For I delight in the law of God after the inward man.*"*

How is this converted Jew who has become a Christian able to say such a thing? How is he able to take delight in the law of the Lord from within his heart, while espousing his newly found faith in Jesus? Especially since in so many of his writings to Christians or churches he founded, he castigates his detractors saying in Galatians 5:1-2, **be not entangled again with the yoke of bondage**.

That was of course a reference to freedom in Christ, from the law-which he asserted to be a **yoke of bondage**. It seems he allows for himself the right to obey and delight in the law, which by the way was the word of God, while allowing himself to delight in and observe Jewish customs and holy days. Yet he attempts to take from fellow Jews the same rights?

In a second verse from Romans 7:25, he shows his thinking, even after his conversion, saying this: **with the mind I myself serve the law of God, but with the flesh, the law of sin**. Writing such things to a Roman thinker, not only negates many scriptures in the Hebrew bible (O.T.), but sets up a scenario which is conducive to lawlessness. Serving the law of God while yet serving the law of sin, is a confusing state of mind.

If the law was the word of God, but his mind was unwilling to follow it, then I understand to some extent what he was saying. But if he was willing and obedient to the law, the power of sin could not prevail over him; for it was written in Psalms 2:1, "***But his delight is in the Law of the Lord, and in it does he meditate day and night***."

This next verse in Romans 8:7 should help us see his dilemma. We know that king David under the "law" in Psalm 2:2, meditated in the law day and night, and was a blessed man, even though he never lived in the times of Jesus, or the Christian era. It doesn't seem unfair to wonder why Paul walked in carnality of the flesh, and was under the power of sin, after knowing Jesus and being filled with the Holy Spirit.

But in the writings of David while under the law, David admits to not being a sinner. David was not a scorner, or sinner, but considered himself successful and prosperous, as opposed to the ungodly. At those times it does not seem that David was affected by carnal flesh, which Paul mentioned as follows. "***Because the carnal mind is enmity against God: for it is not subject unto the law of God,***

neither indeed can be."

Wow! Paul's own Christian writings show how that carnal minded people are the ones who refuse to subject themselves to Gods words or teaching, since their nature forbids acceptance of the Law of God. Who would have thought that "carnal minds" is what prevents people from accepting the word of God (the law), as a rule of faith?

Hostility exists between mankind and God because of the evil inclination. This cannot be changed since the balanced inclination of good was made within every human by the creator. The existence of good and evil is what gives freedom to choose. God did not make the first man a religious robot, He placed within him the ability and power to choose.

The glory of it is that God can work within the power of good, which He prefers, but he can also work His will in spite of the power of evil. Halleluyah! God's commands and words demand response from his creatures, yet the evil inclination which Paul called carnal, is the culprit, but normal mankind still has the power to choose.

This indicates to me, that only the spiritual minded ones will obey, since they have chosen good over evil, and in such a case, God sends grace to that person. Evil exists because the Lord God created it for His reasons.

It was written in Isaiah 45:7; "I form the light, and create darkness: I make peace, and create evil: I YHVH do all these things."

The only reason that evil or bad exists in my opinion, is so that we can choose, for God is pleased when we choose to revere His words. I once heard a modern media preacher say before a potential audience of millions, that God did not create evil, in spite of the fact that a hearer had sent him the verse in Isaiah 45:7. He vehemently insisted again that God did not create anything bad or evil. He attributed all evil to the Devil. So I suppose that he thinks the Devil is co-equal with God, and self-existent from the beginning.

Both humans and angels were given the power to choose. Otherwise the devil who was cast down to earth in Revelation chapter 12, could not have been able to deceive a third part of the angels, who were also cast out of the heaven with him (12:9).

Lest any doubt that the Greek form that was rendered the "ten commandments" was not the Greek terms for τους δεκα λογους, *the ten commandments*, just observe Deuteronomy 10:4, and know that the same term (*nomos*) is used in scripture to refer to "law." Just as the plural forms *logia, logous,* relate to the singular *logos.* Likewise the term *nomos* can relate to or link to any type of *law or command.*

Let's look at Romans 8:4. "That the righteousness of <u>the law</u> might be fulfilled in us, who walk not after the flesh, but after the Spirit."

Our flesh - (σαρχ), had been placed under a death sentence by the Creator. This is due to Adam's sin and our sin. But He has provided an escape from sin's consequences. He supplied the Spirit of life through His son. Once again the Greek New Testament term for law is νομος = *nomos* (Strong's # 3551).

This verse is my major focus point, from Romans 8:7, "***Because the carnal mind is <u>enmity</u> against God; for it is <u>not subject to the law of God</u>, neither indeed can be.***" Enmity means hostility.

The Greek word *nomos* is used again and rendered law. This statement shows why we do not obey the word God has spoken; **the law**. It's because of our unwillingness to subject ourselves to His word's and teachings. That is precisely why Adam and Eve were deceived in the garden of Eden. They were unwilling to believe and obey only one commandment; **the word of God.**

I suggest, based on the writings of Apostle Paul's own words in Romans 8:7, that is the reason why Christians are unable or unwilling to deem the law of the Lord, as essential for them to embrace and keep; is because of **a carnal mind**.

We have been duped into thinking that "the law" is not, and was not the **word of God**. Why has that common Christian viewpoint been formulated?

Did it have anything to do with New Testament writings of the apostles? Just because we were not born under the law, as Jesus was, does that give us a right to defy his plain statements about the law? Notice Matthew 5:18; ***"Think not that I am come to destroy the law*** (νομος) ***or the prophets: I am not come to destroy, but to observe."***

This word "observe" is a better choice than **fulfill**. In the Jewish community, observing was required of every true man who wished to take upon himself the yoke of the commandments, the yoke of God's rule in a young man's life, beginning with bar Mitzvah.

Our King James version bible, wrote in Matthew 5:18, the terms; ***till all be fulfilled***, from the Greek manuscript copy (εως αν παντα γενηται), which literally means;

till all things occur. The permanency of the *nomos (law)*, for the Jew is to be for as long as heaven and earth are standing. In that regard, not the tiniest stroke or decorative extension of any Hebrew letter will pass away.

The very fact that Jesus begins his comment by saying; ***Think not that I am come to destroy the law or the prophets***: should settle the matter for anyone who has doubts about the words of the heavenly Father, and the eternal nature of the word of God.

A different Greek word is used by the text of Matthew 5:17, where Jesus is reported to have said; ***I am not come to destroy, but to fulfill***. That Greek word is πληρωσαι (Strong's Greek #4137). We should understand this to mean compliance on the part of Jesus to the law of the Lord, until the matters prophesied in and under the law and the prophets, should come to pass. Prophecy must be fulfilled regarding the "anointed" or the messianic plan culminates, and that word of fulfillment brings proof. So, every prophetic fulfillment of scripture must occur, and meanwhile, the observance of the law will be practiced by any anointed messenger whom is sent of God (1Peter 2:22).

Notice Matthew 5:18 "For verily I say unto you, Till heaven and earth pass, one jot or one tittle shall in no wise pass from the law, till all be fulfilled."

This verse, when using the terms, **the law**, is actually underscored by Jesus with a Hebrew "amen" (אָמֵן) within a Greek text (αμην). What is a pure Hebrew word doing in a Greek text with a narrative about Jesus? I suggest that it points to a Hebrew narrative, rather than an actual Greek one.

This occurs in all the four Gospels, with over 100 instances in Matthew, Mark, Luke, and John. English readers only see "amen" at the end of each Gospel book, and another at the close of the so called Lord's prayer. This makes only 5 amens, but Greek manuscript copy readers find that Hebrew word embedded over 100 times in the 4 Gospels alone. The same discovery was made years ago by scholars.

English bibles usually render it "verily" or "truly." Amen is not a Greek word, rather it is transliterated perfectly into Greek from the actual Hebrew sounds. The generous use of "amen" throughout the New Testament manuscripts is quite indicative of what would be expected from the native Hebraic speaker, as is the example in numerous verses of the law and in the prophets.

Our English grammar experts of 1611 AD, when translating our bibles overlooked that fact.

Why was Jesus using the "amen" when talking about the law and prophets? Look at the verse **before** the amen, and you will grasp how the Hebraic amen was used.

The Spirit of God teaches those who have listened to any preacher or minster, *that the "amen" comes after something is said of an agreeable nature.* The amen shows the attitude of Jesus about the "law." That term in the Greek language among Hellenist Jews, was the word nomos, which was also used in Greek translation of the Septuagint from the Hebrew language years before Jesus was born into this world (see Deuteronomy 30:10, where the very Hebrew word Torah was translated nomos, as so done in Joshua 1:8), etc., etc.

Jesus' point of focus for listeners to his words was; *"**Think not that I am come to destroy the law, or the prophets**"* (Matthew 5:17). He continues to speak: *"**I am not come to destroy, but to fulfil**."* Our Greek manuscript copy uses the term *kataluo* (Strong's Concordance #2647), which means; *unloose, loosen.* Thus, a proper English translation would be: **Think not that I am come to unloose the law or the prophets**.

For the Jew, it was said by Moses in Deuteronomy 29:29, "The secret things belong unto YHVH our God: but those things which are revealed belong unto us and to our children <u>for ever</u>, that we may do all the words of this law."

Our Greek Old Testament copies wrote *aionoa*, which elsewhere in the Greek New Testament is rendered "everlasting" (John 3:16.). The *nomos* (**law**), from the Greek translation perspective is <u>eternal</u> or <u>everlasting</u> for the Jewish people.

As a matter of fact, this same Greek word rendered **for ever** in the Greek Old Testament is translated various ways in the New Testament, such as; **everlasting**, **eternal**, and **for ever**. For verification purposes the Strong's numbers are 165 and 166. Please run the references and check these comments for accuracy.

God's word and His law, hold all those nuances, but we Christians have been told so often that Jesus kept all the laws on our behalf, that a danger of gross immorality is invading the lives of many who claim to be "saved." No minister or teacher has the right to belittle or demean the words of God in the Old Testament. They are to be reverenced and respected by all, if they wish to be great in the Kingdom of God. Jesus made that absolutely clear according to his words in Matthew 5:19.

"<u>Whosoever</u> therefore shall break one of these least commandments, and shall teach men so, he shall be called least in the kingdom of heaven: but <u>whosoever</u> shall do and and teach [them], the same shall be called great in the kingdom of heaven."

We should consider those words of Jesus, and place them alongside what preachers teachers and authors are saying about Christian theological positions, regarding "the law."

Jesus talked about "<u>breaking</u> the least commandment of the law." Dare we examine the meaning of the word <u>break</u>? Yes, we should investigate it's meaning. Let us look at *lusay* (Strong's 3089, = *release, loosen*). This word sometimes has a meaning of 'breaking destructively, breaking commandments by infringing them, loosing the force of them, rendering them to be non-binding." The cross of Jesus did not release us of moral responsibility simply because we have embraced the new found faith.

Jesus did not die for us that we may continue to sin. Christians have died to sin according to Paul, just as Jesus died for sinners.

Jesus is reported to have used the Greek word *entolay* which our King James scholars rendered **commandments** (Strong's Greek # 1785), an *injunction, charge, precept, commandment.*

It's synonymous with the Hebrew terms *Torah*;

(תּוֹרָה)

and *mitzvah* (מִצְוָה) in the Old Testament.

And what about the use of the word **least** in Matthew 5:19 ? its Greek form *elachistos* (# 1646), simply means "little." A King James dictionary or a concordance relate its meanings as follows: *size, amount, importance, authority of commandments, estimation, activities or operations, very small thing.*

Putting that understanding into motion, indicates the real attitude of Jesus about "the law," the word of his Heavenly Father. Jesus had twice mentioned the word "least" in his comments. First in regard to the **least commandment**, and second in regard to anyone to be considered **least in the kingdom of heaven**.

He was linking those comparisons to those who **teach men so**. Our Greek New Testament word behind "teach" is διδαξη in Strong's Concordance # 1322, *instruction, doctrine.*

Teaching against the writings of Moses and the prophets, puts one into a category of **least** in the kingdom of God, if we are to truly accept the words of Jesus as the basis of our belief system.

Those who **teach and do** [the commandments] are regarded to be the **greatest** (*megas*) in the kingdom of God. But we are also warned by Jesus, that unless ones righteousness exceeds that of hypocritical scribes or Pharisees, they shall in no case enter into the kingdom of heaven.

Those of us in the Gentile Christian community, find those words of Jesus a little disturbing, since in later times, apostle Paul, who was so resisted by Jews refusing to follow Jesus, had made so many disparaging statements about Paul's gospel, that Paul retaliated against them. His teachings aroused many suspicions about him and his followers, and to Jews, it appeared, they were pulling away from Judaism. We are forced to admit that "hypocrisy" must surely have been a general situation among some Jewish leaders in his time, for the ministry of Jesus indicated that some suspicion and hypocrisy existed in his crowds as well.

Surely all Jews were not hypocrites in that day. Mary's husband Joseph was just and devout, Zecharias and Elizabeth, parents of John the baptizer, were *both righteous before God, and walking in all the commandments and ordinances of the Lord blameless* (Luke 1:6).

So much could be said based on New Testament adherents statements, about people not being able to "keep the law," which actually refutes some New Testament comments. It has been said that, **nobody could ever keep the law**. How many times have I heard preachers and teachers insist such falsity with vociferous language? Beside all this, it was written of Jesus, that *"he did no sin, and guile was not found in his mouth"* (1Peter 2:22).

The inability of some people to comprehend that Jesus of Nazareth was able as a man, to keep all the requirements of the law and the prophets, is no excuse that provides forgiveness for non-repentant persons. Otherwise, the body and blood of Jesus on the tree, is blanket forgiveness for even the demons who believe. Nonsense!!!

Repentance is the first fruit of true faith. Luke's Gospel, according to Jesus own words wrote: "Repentance and remission of sins must be preached beginning at Jerusalem and among all nations in his name (Luke 24:47) And ye are witnesses of these things." Only the author of Luke's Gospel claims perfect understanding of all things from the very first (Luke 1:3).

These gospel related words from the mouth of Jesus show that a message to the nations (Gentiles), in no way diminished the power of the law or observance of the words of God, as given to the Jews. Paul's theology was developed <u>after</u> the apostles of Jesus were sent, as well as <u>after</u> the outpouring of the Holy Spirit, which means that Jewish Christians were yet keeping the law, before Paul was ever saved.

Besides churches of today, lean on all Paul's writings for theology, while rejecting his writings about women preaching and teaching, and the relevance of the law, as also being the word of God. His adaptation of the message of the cross, as being his gospel, ignores the thousands and thousands of Jews, Samaritans, and Italians (Acts 10), being saved and Spirit filled, before Saul called Paul, was ever Christianized.

In finding Paul's words a basis for much Christian church theology, we can only wonder why, his attitude about women and their role in speaking under the inspiration of the Holy Ghost, was so strong. Didn't the prophet Joel mention an outpouring of the Holy Spirit upon "all flesh," and upon Jewish sons and "daughters?"

Didn't the law also say "handmaidens." Yet in Paul's letters regarding the church at Corinth, he uses "the law" as a means of avoiding confusion caused by women in that assembly, saying; **as also says the law** to enforce his word relative to **let your women** (wives) **keep silence in** the **churches** (plural). In First Corinthians 14:34. He even goes as far as to say, **the things that I write unto you are the commandments of the Lord**. The Greek term for commandments is *entole* #1725), which is the same Greek term written in Matthew 5:19, and rendered "law." Jesus used the same term in Matthew 5:19, in regard to the *law*.

The *entole* (# 1785) word (commandment), is found frequently in the 4 gospel writings. In the Greek New Testament it is used of both moral and religious precepts, and the same Greek term is found in the ancient Greek Old Testament. Both Exodus 15:26 and Exodus 24: 12 use the Greek form *entolais* and *entolas*, which are plural, and link to commandments and law.

I have found evidence from the Old Testament Greek that both terms *nomos* and *entole* are written in one verse, which uses English words law and commandments (Exo. 24:12). The question arises then; How does Paul's **entole** and **nomos**, fit into the framework of the same words used by God, Moses, and Jesus (according to Old Testament Greek accounts). A comparative analysis does not seem to balance itself. How does one replace the law which God gave to Israel, and nail it to the cross; and then make a law to restrict the activity of the Holy Spirit among wives in the church? How is it, that manmade laws replace what Old Testament prophets had spoken and written? Such things should not be.

Since Jesus did not come to destroy and negate the words of God and Moses, we are forced to conclude that Christian Gentiles should not try to negate or demean the words of Moses and Jesus. Being a follower of Jesus does not turn such persons into "lawless or anti-law" proclaimer. If we would be like Jesus, we should uphold the words and sayings of the Heavenly Father. Just like the good Jew, who believes that the Old Testament is the word of God, and although he may not be a devout and obedient soul, he never denies the reality of the sounds of Sinai. His heritage links to the word **remember**, and it recalls the shofar sound, the smoke and fire, and the mountain quaking. The LORD descended upon Sinai and spoke. It was there on Sinai. that Almighty God spoke, and it was there where God first wrote.

I began to realize due to my studies about the law and its influence on Jesus, and in the four Gospels, that I would search and examine how may gospel verses would show the term **the law**. After collecting some verses with those terms, I decided not to search on the singular word **law**, since there were so many. I had to finish this particular writing. The English search terms are **the law** (from my computer based bible version).

My computer search phrase is **the law**, with verses located first in the Gospel of Matthew, and continuing to the other Gospels. My searching phrase found <u>9 verses</u> containing words, **the law**. See Matthew 5:17, 5:18, 5:40, 7:12, 11:13, 12:5, 22:36, 22:40, and Matthew 22:43. We found 2 Greek forms, one is κρινο, Strong's # 2919, found in Matthew 5:40, and the other 8 verses use the Greek term νομος, Strong's # 3551.

The use of *krino* in Matthew 5:40 involves a legal verdict, such as a judgment by the court. The uses of ***nomos*** in the other verses follow this pattern;

1. *Writings of Old Testament prophets*

2. *Strokes of Hebrew or Greek alphabet letters*

3. *Respectful consideration of others as taught by the law and the prophets*

4. *All the spokespersons that prophesied under the law and before John the Baptist*

5. *Group of writings, inclusive of Sabbath day teachings and priestly laws pertaining to the Temple, great commandment written in the law*

6. *Two great commandments upon which the law and the prophets hang*

7. *Judgment mercy and faith,*

8. *The weightier matters of the law*

In Mark's Gospel; I found no uses of the English translation terms; **the law**. That precise search term produced no results. Surprise!

In Luke's Gospel - I was able to locate (10) verses in Luke's Gospel with the exact English terms; **the law**. Let's begin with Luke 2:22, 2:23, 2:24, 2:27, 2:39, 5:17, 10:26, 16:16, 16:17, and Luke 24:44. These verses about the law, use the same Greek word nomos Strong's # 3551, which I shared from the Gospel of Matthew.

In these verses **the law**:

Involves religious writings about purification

Is called this time the law of Moses

Teachings about firstborn

Sacrifices specified by the word of God

Laws about new born, specified law of the Lord

Teachers of the law of the Lord

Observance of the law of the Lord leading to eternal life

A comparison of heaven and earth passing away before the failing of the smallest detail in an alphabet letter.

Division of the law into three segments; the law of Moses, the prophets, and the <u>writings</u> (or Psalms).

In the Gospel of John, I found the English terms **"the law"** in 7 verses. My first find was John 1:17, then in John 1:45, 7:19, 7:23, 7:49, 8:5, and John 12:44.

The 7 verses in John's Gospel relate first of all, that **the law** was given by Moses, but grace and truth was given by Jesus Christ (John 1:17). This comment by the author of John, didn't imply that the law was not the truth, nor that grace was not existent under the law of Moses. It was designed to show that the revelation of Jesus the Christ, who is the glory of God (1:14), dwelt among humans as the only begotten of the Father, and he was **full of grace and truth**.

John 1:45 asserts that, **"We have found him of whom Moses in the law, and the prophets, did write."** Philip tells Nathaniel that it is **Jesus of Nazareth**. This means that certain segments of Jewish writings in the law, point to Jesus, although his name is not mentioned in the writings. In John 7:19, Jesus points out that some Jerusalem Jews **sought to kill him** (John 7:1), but he accused the Jews at that feast of not keeping **the law** of Moses, because of murderous intentions in their heart, by going about to **kill me**.

In John 7:23, we read that **nomos** (law), consists of matters such as Sabbath day and circumcision, and are teachings of the word of God as given to Moses. In John 7:49, Some Pharisees who did not believe in Jesus said; ***this people who know not the law are cursed***. But Nicodemus being a devout Jew and a leader, defended against the Pharisees words saying;

"Does our law judge any man, before it hear him, and knows what he does?"

The example of two Jews exist in this verse, one who is a Pharisee, and hypocritical, the other a Jew who refuses to pass judgment until the facts are shown (John 7:51).

John 8:5 gives an example regarding a woman supposedly taken in adultery. I use the term supposedly, because the partner to the woman is not present, since they were taken in the act. When is an adulterous man innocent, but a woman is guilty? Secondly, an adulterous person cannot be stoned without a trial, and the witnesses must be the first to begin the stoning, according to the law of Moses. See Leviticus 20:10, and Deuteronomy 22:22. There are also writings of Moses which mention the requirement of two witnesses. It is evident that those scribes and Pharisees did <u>not know the law of Moses</u>.

Our final verse in John 12:34, containing the English terms **the law**, is found to say; *we have heard out of the law that Christ abides for ever*.

Such a conclusion or statement must have some written verses to verify that, since it was written "**out of the law**." I only find hints that relates such to the Son of man, David, or a son of David. They are found in Psalm 89:36-37, Psalm 110:4, Isaiah 9:7, Ezekiel 37:25, and Daniel 7:14. None of them mention Christ, although in Christian theology, it is considered to be that the son of man, the anointed one is also the son of David. Yet, I did find in the Greek Septuagint version of the Old Testament the terms of Psalm 89:38 - χριστον σου (*your christ = your anointed*). Perhaps, they had read the Greek translation term "christ" (anointed), and linked it to the Hebrew "mashiach."

I had located <u>26</u> Gospel verses in the writings of Matthew, Mark, Luke, and John with the precise English phrase, the law. That in itself is somewhat of interest to me, since the Divine and primary name of the God of Israel, YHVH, is equal to the number 26. That **gemaria is quite revealing.**

This number value of the Divine and proper name of Israel's God, and the God of Abraham, Isaac and Jacob, the one who gave **the law**, is equaled by 26 Gospel verses which contain the precise number of verses which equate that Divine name. Interesting indeed, since no person could have possibly known beforehand that such would be the case.

Our journey through biblical humility in the church, an example of a humble man, sobriety, attitudes about grace under the law and gospel, and its impact on a trend of lawless behavior will end here.

It's my hope that every reader will have a greater respect for the section of our bible called the Old Testament. It's the only bible that early first century believers in Jesus had known or read before 33 AD.

GLOSSARY

This list of terms encountered by the reader of this book, will have some definitions or explanations to assist them in understanding. **They are shown in order as appearing in each chapter**.

Shekinah - a Hebrew word depicting the Divine Presence of God, thought by some rabbis to represent the feminine aspect of Deity. The Hebrew root form is found in numerous bible verses, but the first mention is in Exodus 25:8, שָׁכַן).

Holy One - Found in 45 Old Testament verses and mostly related to the LORD (YHVH), as "Holy One of Israel. A reflection of monotheism. There are 6 New Testament verses employing the phrase "holy one" (of God), as a reference to Jesus.

Sotah 4b - A tractate in the Mishnah, with teachings or repetitions on the subject of women.

Pesachim 66b - A tractate in the Mishnah with teachings about festivals such as Passover.

Trance - a half conscious state between

sleeping and waking.

Similitude - Likeness, or resemblance. In the Hebrew bible, from terms like דְמוּת *d'mooth,* Genesis 1:26.

Greek characters (letters) - showing in the actual Greek form with corresponding English spelling in Italics. In some cases a Strong's Concordance number is given for follow up, with definitions.

Greek Septuagint - A Greek language translation made from the Hebrew Bible. It is dated around 200-300 years before the coming of Jesus. It originated from Alexandria, Egypt.

LORD - In earliest complete English bibles (1611 AD), this capitalized word "LORD" was translated from the Hebrew letters יהוה equated with English matching letter sounds YHVH. Modern English and modern Hebrew letter matching sounds are the letters YHVH. There are no vowel sounds in Hebrew, but were designed to help the uninitiated reader.

YHVH - A transliteration effort to accurately reflect the proper and Divine name of the God of Israel, with English letter sounds. The form of which יהוה, is said to occur around 6,823 times in the Old Testament. A translation and transliteration of Isaiah 42:8 shows the reality: I am YHVH; that is My name: and My glory will I not give to another, neither My praise to graven images.

Adage - Traditional saying representing a common observation or experience.

Verbiage - Overabundance of words in writing or speech.

Good tidings, glad tidings - These two translation terms occur in our New Testament in Luke 1:19 and Luke 2:10, with Greek terms ευαγγελιζω, Strong's Concordance #2097 and elsewhere in New Testament writings they were rendered with the word gospel. In Luke's 2 verses they were tidings announced about the birth of two baby boys. This indicates that the word Gospel is not always focused around the death, burial, and resurrection of Jesus.

Companion verse - A different account from another writer which corroborates or confirms an event.

Manuscript - A document made from an original (called an autograph). In 1989 AD, there was reported to be 5,366 manuscripts of the New Testament.

Yisrael -The "Y" letter in English

correctly matches for the Hebrew name (Israel). This is also true regarding the "J" sound in Jesus, Jordan, Jehovah, Jerusalem, etc. The "J" sound happened because of an English language shift. Manuscript copies do not confirm the "J" tradition.

Hashem - A Hebrew bible word meaning "the name," by which Jewish tradition allows for protection of the sacred name יהוה. From their perspective it is a respectful way of obeying Exodus 20:7.

Apar-ne' om-ahee - English letter sounds in short syllables showing how to pronounce a Greek word and where to accentuate (απαρνε–ομαι).

Capernaum - The name of a "village" in Israel, possibly linked to the identity of the prophet Nahum.

Zion - Properly Tzion, an area on the Temple Mount in Jerusalem, and according to the Book of Psalm's 48:2-3, the Mount of His holiness, the city of the great King, the joy of the whole earth.

Foal - The nursing young of any mammal of the horse family.

Ass - Also known as a donkey.

Theology - A field of study related to God and His attributes. From the Greek words Theos and logia.

Universal Church - A term representing the Catholic or organized and wide extended Christian body.

Jezebel and Nicolas - representative of false doctrines and persons named by the Holy Spirit in churches of Asia as mentioned in Revelation 2:6, 2:15, and Revelation 2:20.

Book of Jacob - A corrected reference to the Book of James of Christian tradition. The Greek manuscript words call for Jacob, not James. After over 400 years of this err, it's time that somebody restored the man his actual and true name based on manuscript copies. The glaring error of certain verses show the intellectual dishonesty of someone, as known by the reading, The God of Abraham, and of Isaac, and of [Jacob], elsewhere translated James. See Acts 3:13, and Acts 7:32 where the Greek form calls for a (Ιακωβ) or (Ιακωβος) transliteration. # 2384, 2385.

Parable - Same as the word Proverb, where something is laid alongside, for comparative analysis to promote understanding.

Atone - Originating from a biblical word

כָּפַר), *kaphar*; to cover. The religious concept is to cover sins. Old timers used to explain in simple terms make at one (atone) with God. Generally speaking, in the Hebrew scriptures, it was done through the blood of innocent animals, specified by Moses' writings.

Passover - A God given Jewish holy day, when national deliverance from Egyptian bondage was celebrated. The biblical name is Pesach. Its commemoration is once a year for ever.

Charedim - Tremblers (when hearing the word of God). See Isaiah 66:5.

Negative consequences - retribution for doing something forbidden by God.

Negative injunction - A negative or shall not command given by the Lord.

Strait Gate - A narrow passage or gate.

Justification - in Greek New Testament manuscripts the word means: to declare righteous, acquittal. In Christian doctrine it involves righteousness being imputed to the believer because of the death of Jesus the Christ.

Repentance - a change of the mind with Godly sorrow, regarding sin and wrong doing. A desire to turn to God's teaching.

Remission of sins - Promised under John the Baptists ministry, as well as to earliest followers of Jesus' teachings. Even those complicit in the death of Jesus, received the promise of forgiveness and the Holy Spirit baptism in Acts 2:39.

Blasphemy - From a Greek bible word meaning; to speak against; to revile.

Scriptures - In Jesus day it meant all the writings of Moses and the prophets, for up until his death, only the Old Testament writings were considered thus. After the resurrection of Jesus, authors took upon themselves to write and spread the news. Today, Christians accept both Old and New Testament writings as scripture.

Heretical - A professing believer who speaks religious opinions contrary to organized church doctrine.

Oodles and bookoos - Slang terms for "bunches and gobs" of something.

Gentile - Any non-Jewish person or nation.

Holy Ghost - better translated as "Holy

Spirit." In the Old Testament the English terms used were, Spirit of the Lord, Spirit of God. Jesus identified God as A Spirit in John 4:24.

Apostolic Decree - Something decided and promoted by the handpicked and selected apostles of Jesus. Sometimes letters were sent by the mother church in Jerusalem with decisions on those matters (see Acts 15:23-30).

Paganism - Any individual or group with a characteristic of worshipping more than one deity (polytheism), such as ancient Romans or Greeks.

Carnal nature - In Paul's New Testament writings, it is a reference to the fleshly nature and appetites of the animal like impulse, not governed by the Spirit of God.

Lawlessness - Without regard to law; contrary to law.

Mundane - Worldly as contrasted with heavenly.

Elohim - The generic Hebrew word for God, god, gods, false gods, judges, angels and some humans such as Moses (see Exodus 7:1, and Exodus 4:16).

Torah - Translated as "law," but actually

has meanings of teaching and instruction.

Transliteration, Transliterated - Changing letters or words into corresponding characters of another language or alphabet.

Mitzvah - A bible commandment from the writings   of Moses or the prophets.

Scribe - A person specially trained to write or copy an existing Torah scroll.

Blanket forgiveness - Forgiveness that is granted to everyone or a group, without repentance or godly sorrow. (This writer's attempt to show how ridiculous it is to assume forgiveness without acknowledgement of sin, or without repentance).

Circumcision - A fleshly cut on the male organ and foreskin as was required by the LORD for the sons of Abraham, Isaac, and of Jacob, and all the Sons of Israel. See Genesis 17:9-13 and Genesis 17:19.

Sabbath - A Greek form for the Hebrew Shabbat, meaning rest, or cease. It is the day of rest and cessation from labor, based on first mention in Genesis 2:3. Jews continue to this day, to honor the 7th day as a day of rest.

Christ - A non-Jewish term, that happened beginning with the Greek Septuagint translation of the Hebrew Bible, around 200-300 years before Jesus came into the world. The Hellenist community (Greek) of Alexandria Egypt, may have lost the use of the mother tongue of Hebrew, and required a Greek translation of the bible. Perhaps the ruler of Alexandria wanted a copy in Greek for the royal library. Whatever the reason may be, the Septuagint Greek used terms (χριστω, χριστος), christ, in reference to the word "anointed." Thus, the Hebrew persons of High priests, Saul, David, and Cyrus king of Persia had the Greek writing of christ attached to themselves in Greek scripture. It comes as a shock to many Christians to know this truth, but the facts are indisputable, when one examines the manuscripts. The actual Hebrew words before the Greek Old Testament translation was made are;

מָשִׁיחַ

mashiach, and translated variously with spellings of *messiah, messias.*

Gematria - An interpretive device whereby words are understood through the numerical value of their letters. The Hebrew alphabet letters *alef* through *tet*, represent

148

values 1 through 9. The letters *yud* to *tzadi* represent 10 through 90. The letters *koof* to *tav* represent 100 through 400. Some use the system to uncover biblical truths since the system is very ancient (they are known by the term *Kabbalists*).

TRUTH
Nuggets

Christian Scriptures Compared To

The Original Hebrew Texts

By Ronald L Drown

ABOUT THE AUTHOR

Ronald L. Drown
Biblical Hebrew Teacher and
Author of "The Real Jesus" and "Truth Nuggets"

Ron desires that you gain an accurate insight and deeper knowledge of the life and teachings of Yeshua. After pastoring for many years, Ron founded YAD-EL as a result of his love for Israel, extensive research and study of the Hebrew language and Biblical translations, Hebrew thought, Ancient Sacred Writings and Texts, as well as Judaism.

Ron now aims to bridge the understanding of the Jewish Tradition and Christianity's Jewish Roots and rich heritage, to people of faith from all walks of life. He holds seminars and group classes for those interested in learning to write, read, and understand Sephardic Hebrew (Biblical Hebrew and modern Hebrew).

The late Robert L Lindsay, Scholar, Author, Founder of "The Jerusalem Perspective," and Pastor in Jerusalem for 47 years, highly commended Ronald for his translation of "The Gospel of Mark," from Hebrew to English.

His knowledge of the Hebrew Biblical text has both practicality and depth. His familiarity with Jewish traditions which relate well to the Christian faith, allow him to provide rich learning experiences to the Christian community, enhancing the understanding of their religious roots and enriching Biblical studies. His working knowledge of the Greek New Testament is also a valuable help to students of the Bible.

Ron's focus is particular to the Jewish people, as he has a heart for Israel, and provides for ministries such as the Wings of Eagles, who regularly feeds and transports Jewish families back to their homeland from the former Soviet Union.

Ronald is the Founder of the Lighthouse of Jesus Christ, and YAD-EL Ministries. Ronald and his wife Ruth make their home in sunny Florida.

TO LEARN MORE VISIT

WWW.LIGHTHOUSEOFJESUS.ORG

155

RECEIVE YOUR FREE HEBREW PRAYER TODAY AS SEEN IN CHARISMA MAGAZINE:

VISIT WWW.LIGHTHOUSEOFJESUS.ORG
OR SCAN QR CODE WITH YOUR PHONE AS SEEN BELOW

A MONTHLY HEBREW PRAYER WILL BE EMAILED TO YOU FROM
REV RON'S HEBREW PRAYERS SERIES (MP3 DOWNLOAD)

1

SCAN WITH SMART PHONE APP

2

ADD YOUR EMAIL
(Then Follow Confirm Instructions In
Your Email)

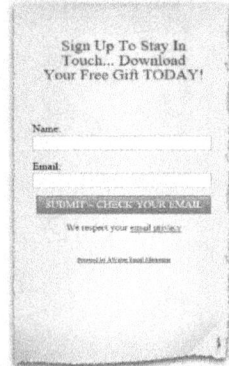

Sign Up To Stay In
Touch... Download
Your Free Gift TODAY!

Name:

Email:

SUBMIT - CHECK YOUR EMAIL

We respect your email privacy

3

LISTEN TO OR DOWNLOAD
YOUR PRAYER
(You Will Receive Your Password/Link
In Your Email)

LightHouse
and YAD-EL MINISTRIES

Protected: Hebrew Prayers ~ #1
~ The Lords Prayer

YAD-EL PODCAST

Biblical Hebrew Studies By Ron Brown

Prayer One ~ Week One

The Lord's Prayer

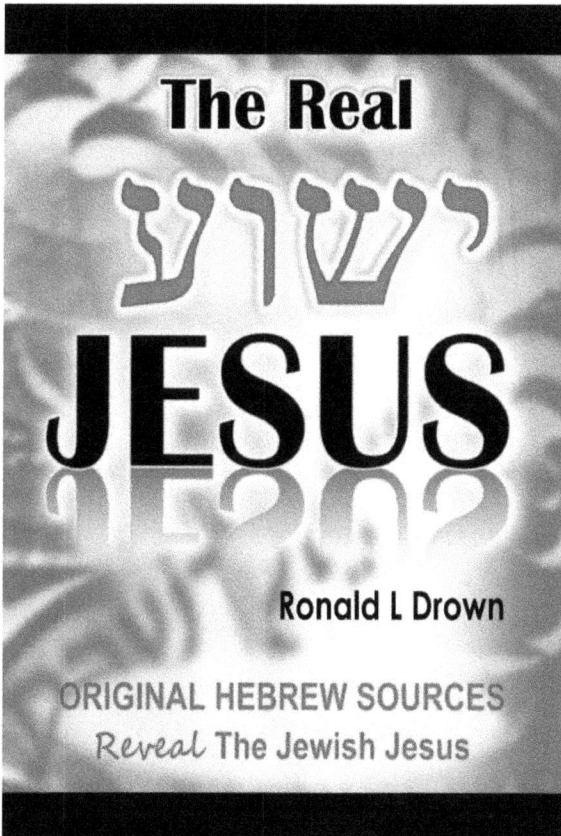

A Prayer Of David

Create in me a clean heart, Oh God;
Renew a right spirit within me.

Cast me not away from thy presence;
And take not thy holy spirit from me.

Restore unto me the joy of thy salvation;
And uphold me with thy free spirit.

Then will I teach transgressors thy ways;
And sinners shall be converted unto thee.

Psalm 51: 10-13

www.ingramcontent.com/pod-product-compliance
Lightning Source LLC
Chambersburg PA
CBHW070331090426
42733CB00012B/2444